PRAISE FOR
The Rock, the Road, and the Rabbi

This is one of those unique "if" books that speaks deep into your soul with promise and possibility. Because *if* you've always wanted to visit the Holy Land, *if* you want a deeper understanding of the Bible, and *if* you enjoy great stories from a great storyteller—then this is a perfect book for you.

—Roma Downey, actor, producer, and president of LightWorkers Media

Kathie Lee Gifford has encouraged and inspired me for many years. This book will do the same for you. She escorts the reader to the land of the Savior, taking us on a heart-deepening journey of hope.

—Max Lucado, pastor and *New York Times* bestselling author

Living one's faith unashamedly and joyfully in the public square as my friend Kathie Lee Gifford has done is rare and beautiful, and has inspired me personally in my own faith. So it's no suprise that this rare and beautiful book should inspire me too. If it doesn't make you want to know God better—and make you want to visit Israel!—you obviously haven't read it yet. What are you waiting for?

—Eric Metaxas, *New York Times* bestselling author of *Bonhoeffer: Pastor, Martyr, Prophet, Spy* and host of the nationally syndicated *Eric Metaxas Show*

Kathie Lee Gifford's vibrant personality is revealed in her book *The Rock, the Road, and the Rabbi.* You can sense the thrill of her many treks through the Holy Land as she writes about its captivating beauty and its spiritually deep roots that have found a place in her heart, all because of the power of God's Word. Take time to read her innermost thoughts as she shares her experiences of walking where Jesus walked. "Seek [God] . . . and find him, though he is not far from any one of us" (Acts 17:27). Fix your heart on the Rock of salvation and walk the Road that leads to redemption with the Rabbi—the teacher who gives eternal life to those who seek Him.

—Franklin Graham, president and CEO, Billy Graham Evangelistic Association and Samaritan's Purse

D0050188

The Bible is probably the single most significant written work in history, and yet it's so often misunderstood, distorted, or overlooked. In *The Rock, the Road, and the Rabbi*, Kathie Lee Gifford does the important work of studying and sharing this most foundational of books, hitting both the mind and the heart with the powerful impact of what she uncovers. I am grateful for what this book has done for my life, and you will be too.

—Allison Pataki, *New York Times* bestselling author of *The Accidental Empress*

The Rock, the Road, and the Rabbi will inspire and uplift readers everywhere. Whether you are a believer or not, a seeker or simply intrigued, this glorious walking tour of the Holy Land, with personal insights and stories by Kathie Lee Gifford, describes the sacred places of Israel and their meaning step by step. Rabbi Jason Sobel offers biblical and historical context with clarity and insight. From the stillness of the desert to the serenity of the Sea of Galilee, you will be swept into the beauty, wonder, and magnificence of these sacred places by two enthusiastic believers on a lifelong faith journey.

—Adriana Trigiani, *New York Times* bestselling author

A personal, inviting, and engaging encounter with both the Jesus of history, the man who walked the dusty landscape of first-century Judea and Galilee, and the Christ of faith, the one around whom the author's entire life revolves. Especially for Christians who know little about Jesus' Jewish background, this book is a fine place to begin your journey.

—James Martin, SJ, *New York Times* bestselling author of *Jesus: A Pilgrimage*

the ROCK, the ROAD, and the RABBI

My Journey *into the* Heart *of* Scriptural Faith *and the* Land Where It All Began

KATHIE LEE GIFFORD

WITH RABBI JASON SOBEL

W PUBLISHING GROUP

AN IMPRINT OF THOMAS NELSON

Published in Nashville, Tennessee, by W Publishing, an imprint of Thomas Nelson.

Photos in the color insert were taken by Benjamin Wierda.

"He Saw Jesus"
Music by Brett James and Lyrics by Kathie Lee Gifford
© 2017, CassyCody Music Ltd (ASCAP) and Cornman Music (ASCAP)
All Rights Reserved. Used by Permission.

"Lead Me, Gentle Shepherd"
Music by David Pomeranz and Lyrics by Kathie Lee Gifford
© 2017, CassyCody Music Ltd (ASCAP) and Upward Spiral Music (ASCAP)
All Rights Reserved. Used by Permission.

Thomas Nelson titles may be purchased in bulk for educational, business, fund-raising, or sales promotional use. For information, please email SpecialMarkets@ThomasNelson.com.

Unless otherwise noted, Scripture quotations are taken from the Holy Bible, New International Version®, NIV®. Copyright © 1973, 1978, 1984, 2011 by Biblica, Inc.® Used by permission of Zondervan. All rights reserved worldwide. www.zondervan.com. The "NIV" and "New International Version" are trademarks registered in the United States Patent and Trademark Office by Biblica, Inc.®

Scripture quotations marked TLV are taken from the Tree of Life Translation of the Bible. Copyright © 2015 by the Messianic Jewish Family Bible Society.

Scripture quotations marked NKJV are from the New King James Version®. © 1982 by Thomas Nelson. Used by permission. All rights reserved.

Scripture quotations marked NLT are from the Holy Bible, New Living Translation. © 1996, 2004, 2007, 2013, 2015 by Tyndale House Foundation. Used by permission of Tyndale House Publishers, Inc., Carol Stream, Illinois 60188. All rights reserved.

Scripture quotations marked NASB are taken from New American Standard Bible®, Copyright © 1960, 1962, 1963, 1968, 1971, 1972, 1973, 1975, 1977, 1995 by The Lockman Foundation. Used by permission. (www.Lockman.org)

Scripture quotations marked ESV are taken from the ESV® Bible (The Holy Bible, English Standard Version®), copyright © 2001 by Crossway, a publishing ministry of Good News Publishers. Used by permission. All rights reserved.

Italics used in Scripture passages are the author's own emphasis, save for material quoted from the TLV translation.

Any Internet addresses, phone numbers, or company or product information printed in this book are offered as a resource and are not intended in any way to be or to imply an endorsement by Thomas Nelson, nor does Thomas Nelson vouch for the existence, content, or services of these sites, phone numbers, companies, or products beyond the life of this book.

ISBN 978-0-7852-2223-1 (SC)
ISBN 978-0-7852-1600-1 (eBook)
ISBN 978-0-7852-2268-2 (special edition)
ISBN 978-0-7852-2287-3 (special edition)

Library of Congress Control Number: 2017956361

ISBN 978-0-7852-1596-7

Printed in the United States of America

20 21 22 23 LSC 10 9

The most important fact I want to emphasize at the beginning of this book is this: *I am not a biblical scholar or an expert in biblical studies*. I am simply a lifetime student of the Word of God and a seeker of truth.

But in my search for a deeper understanding of the Bible, I have met extraordinary people such as my friends Emilie and Craig Wierda, to whom I am most grateful for first inviting me along this amazing journey.

And finally I thank God for Ray Vander Laan, Rod Van Solkema, and Rabbi Jason Sobel, three men who have taken me up steep slopes, led me deep into the desert, explained ancient mysteries, and revealed what Scripture means in its original form. Most importantly, they have relit a passion in my innermost being for the Bible and rekindled my desire for the Lover of my soul: Jesus, the Messiah.

For that I am eternally grateful, and to them I dedicate *The Rock, the Road, and the Rabbi*.

—KATHIE LEE GIFFORD

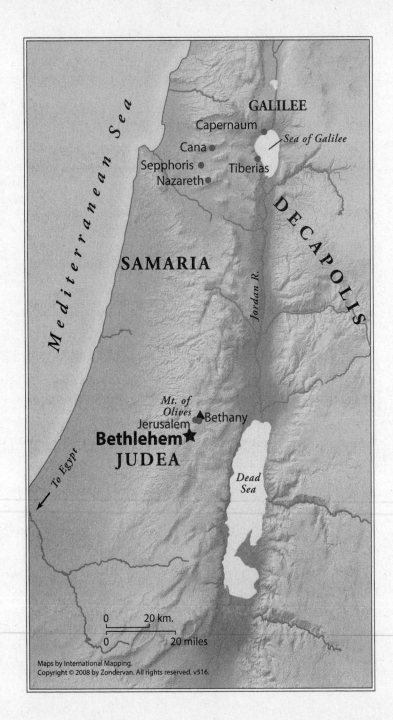

CONTENTS

CONTENTS

INTRODUCTION

Lord, You Want Me to What?

*The steadfast love of the LORD never ceases; his mercies never come
to an end; they are new every morning; great is your faithfulness.*
—LAMENTATIONS 3:22–23 ESV

Before I began my new job as cohost of the fourth hour of *The
Today Show* in 2008, I felt the Lord tugging at my spirit with
the words of Matthew 6:33: *Kathie, seek first My kingdom and My righteousness, and all these things will be given to you as well.*

I remember responding, "Lord, You know that's what I am trying to do—put You and Your kingdom first in my life."

Then I felt Him gently rebuke me: *You're not listening. I said to seek
Me first!*

"Lord, do You mean first thing in the morning before anything
else?" I questioned.

In my heart, I sensed His clear answer: *Yes.*

Wow. I already got up earlier than most—usually right before
dawn. But with my new duties at *Today*, I would be leaving my home

in Connecticut shortly after 6:00 a.m. for the hour-long commute into New York City.

"Really, Lord? Before I go into work?"

Yes. I felt Him tenderly remind me, *As you begin your day, so goes your day.*

So I began to awaken before 4:00 a.m. and pray for an hour for my family members, friends and colleagues, world situations, and personal concerns. Then I would open the Scriptures and study God's Word for an hour more, with my puppies and the birds outside my window as my only company.

This new discipline soon became the best part—and my favorite part—of the day. I began to understand and cherish the Scriptures that talk about the joy of seeking God in the morning:

- "Let the *morning* bring me word of your unfailing love, for I have put my trust in you. Show me the way I should go, for to you I entrust my life" (Psalm 143:8).
- "It is good to praise the LORD and make music to your name, O Most High, proclaiming your love in the *morning* and your faithfulness at night" (Psalm 92:1–2).
- "In the *morning*, LORD, you hear my voice; in the *morning* I lay my requests before you and wait expectantly" (Psalm 5:3).
- "O God, You are my God; *early* will I seek You; my soul thirsts for You; my flesh longs for You in a dry and thirsty land where there is no water" (Psalm 63:1 NKJV).
- "He will make your righteous reward shine like the *dawn*, your vindication like the noonday sun" (Psalm 37:6).
- "The path of the righteous is like the *morning* sun, shining ever brighter till the full light of day" (Proverbs 4:18).

Through this process of getting up early every morning to study God's Word, I have experienced the truth of my favorite Bible verse: "I can do all things through Christ who strengthens me" (Philippians 4:13 NKJV).

Where do we get everything we need in life? From the Lord our God.

How does He strengthen us? With His Word.

Changing my morning routine has changed my life. I began not only to study the Word, but also to memorize as much as I could so that Scripture would become a living, breathing part of me. No textbook needed, no study guide necessary—just the pure, life-giving, sustaining Word of God settled deep in my soul.

Ever since then, I have been passionate about knowing and understanding the Bible. It breaks my heart to watch so many people desperate to find meaning, cures, and answers from a world that only wants to promote products, gain profit, and exploit human need.

Every answer to every question and every single desire and need anyone will ever have is already available for us in God's Word. The problem is that too few people are willing to do the work of searching for it! "Ask and it will be given to you," Jesus tells us. "Seek and you will find; knock and the door will be opened to you" (Matthew 7:7). In other words, make an effort!

Many of us have become so complacent, spoiled, and comfortable that we don't realize we are miserable. Isaiah 55:2 says: "Why spend money on what is not bread, and your labor on what does not satisfy? Listen, listen to me, and eat what is good, and you will delight in the richest of fare." I believe this is how our faith grows stale, our joy diminishes, and our passion for God runs dry.

We know that eventually we will die if we don't eat food. But we will all die spiritually if we stop feeding on His Word! "*Taste* and see that the LORD is good," Psalm 34:8 says. When we fill our lives with everything but the very thing we need most to thrive in our faith—His Word—we become lukewarm. We become bored and indifferent. We fall out of love with God.

One of my favorite verses is Psalm 18:30: "As for God, his way is perfect: The LORD's word is flawless." Friends, this is either a fact or a lie. There is no middle ground.

This is why I have grown so passionate about learning what the Bible really says. If I am going to base my life on something, it has to be the truth, the whole truth, and nothing but the truth, so help me, God! But how can we live the truth if we don't even know it?

Granted, there are mysteries in Scripture that will remain mysterious because God wills them to. But Jesus said in John 8:32, "You will know the truth, and the truth will set you free." Even Pontius Pilate asked Jesus, "What is truth?" (John 18:38).

Everyone wants to know what truth is, but too often in our world the truth is manipulated by individuals, organizations, or the media to accomplish certain agendas. It seems impossible to wade through all the informational garbage.

The word *truth* occurs in the Bible more than two hundred times. Obviously, God places immeasurable value in the truth, and He longs for each of us to seek it, find it, and apply it to our lives. The Bible is our treasure map. We can use its parables, psalms, numbers, prophecies, and personal stories of faith to guide our understanding. But this process requires great effort on our part. All too often we are so overwhelmed by technology, our personal dramas, and our endless ambition that we neglect to study God's Word. Imagine how it breaks the heart of our heavenly Father—who loves His children and longs to lead us into all joy, peace, and hope—when He sees us putting all our energy into everything but the one thing that can bring us life.

One of the saddest things I've encountered through the years when I try to share the gospel of salvation through Jesus, the Messiah, as taught in the Bible, is that many people dismiss the message immediately because of what they have already heard and therefore believe about what the Bible says.

They say they can't put their faith in a book that maintains the earth was created in seven days. They say they can't put their faith in a vengeful God who wants mankind to fear His judgment or they'll be sent to hell. They hate the apostle Paul's admonition for wives to be submissive to their husbands. They refuse to even pick up a Bible, read it, or study it in any way, even though most reasonable people agree it is the single most influential piece of literature ever written in all of history.

When people share their concerns with me, I always respond in the same way: "You have to understand what the Bible actually says, not what you've been told by others who are usually misinformed."

For instance, the word in Genesis 1:1–5 translated "day" is the Hebrew word *yom*, which refers to a period of time with a beginning and an end. It is unlikely it was a twenty-four-hour solar day, because the sun, moon, and stars do not appear until the fourth "day."

As to the issue of fearing God, I thought it would be fascinating to look up what the word *fear* actually means in ancient Hebrew.

I discovered that the word *yirah*, translated "fear," has a range of meanings.

In Jewish thought, there are three levels of fear. First, there is the fear of punishment or pain (*yirat ha'onesh*).[1] This is the sense in which we usually think of the word *fear*. Second, there is the fear of breaking God's law (*yirat ha'malkhut*).[2] This is the fear of being punished by God for sin. The third type of fear is a deep reverence for and awareness of the presence of God (*yirat ha'rommemnut*): "The fear of the LORD leads to life; then one rests content, untouched by trouble" (Proverbs 19:23).[3] This is the healthy type of fear that draws us near to God. "There is no fear in love. But perfect love drives out fear, because fear has to do with punishment. The one who fears is not made perfect in love" (1 John 4:18). If we "fear" God in this way, then we will be aware of God's presence all around us. I love this thought!

On the subject of submission, I thought it would be interesting to test what I had been learning from my rabbinic study and go to the original text. I searched for what "submit" means in the original text of Ephesians 5:22, where Paul exhorts, "Wives, submit yourselves to your own husbands as you do to the Lord." I found the Greek word *hupotasso*. Basically, it means "to identify with" or "to be in support of." This is different from the English translation, which is taken from the Greek word *hupeiko*, meaning "submit to."

The biblical meaning of submission has nothing to do with being a doormat or a second-class citizen, or even a slave of any kind. Instead, it seems to point to what most of Jesus' teaching points to: be kind to one another, love one another, be of service to one another, and treat others the way you want to be treated.

The truth is that some people aren't aware of the facts about

God's Word, and others choose to ignore them. The Bible is not an ancient, dead book. Hebrews 4:12 tells us, "The word of God is alive and active."

God is a covenant-keeping, faithful, unchanging Father to us all in a world where everything else changes from one moment to the next.

In this book you will have the exciting opportunity to discover the *truth* of the Bible and learn what many passages in the Scriptures really mean. You will experience the Rock (Jesus), the Road (the Holy Land), and the Rabbi (the Word of God) as you have never experienced them before!

Come deeper as we explore the land of Israel and mine the treasures of God's Word together. There is so much more!

PREFACE

My Love Affair with Israel

Pray for the peace of Jerusalem:
"May they prosper who love you."
—PSALM 122:6 NASB

My love affair with the land of Israel began the moment I took my very first step onto the Promised Land in June of 1971. I was seventeen years old, and my father's high school graduation gift was a trip for me and my mother to attend the first Jerusalem Conference on Biblical Prophecy. I missed my graduation ceremony, but I couldn't have cared less. I was where it all happened! All the stories I had heard, all the Scriptures I had studied since I was a young girl—*everything* I believed from the Word of God had taken place thousands of years before in this land I was experiencing for the very first time! That thought took my breath away all those years ago. It still does today.

I have returned to Israel many times during the last forty-five years, and each time I have come back a totally transformed person.

Why? you might ask. *What is so magical about a small piece of rocky terrain roughly the size of New Hampshire that gives it the power to completely redirect, redefine, and ultimately redeem a human heart?*

That question is the essence of this book. I want to take you to the Holy Land. I want you to experience the thrill of discovering the Word of God in its original languages of Hebrew and Greek, because I believe with all my soul that the answer to every question any person will ever ask is hidden in that land and in the Word of God in its purest form.

Come! Let's go to the land, let's hear the Word, and let's be transformed by the wonder of it all.

Meet the Good Rabbi: Jason Sobel

I first met Rabbi Jason Sobel in December 2016 during the Christmas rush at Rockefeller Center. I had heard about him for several years from friends I respect very much, and to a person, their regard for him and the depth of his teaching was extraordinary. "You *have* to meet him!" my friends told me. "His teaching will change your life."

So Jason and I sat across from each other at my favorite New York City restaurant, Neary's Pub, and ordered the famous lamb chops. I instantly warmed to him. Rabbi Jason is the kind of person who gives you a big smile and a bear hug that leaves you breathless.

I expressed to Rabbi Jason my exasperation with what Christmas has deteriorated into: a massive, crass, commercial circus that has nothing to do with the birth of Jesus Christ. I challenge anyone to find a baby in a manger anywhere! (Okay, they still have one at the end of the Christmas Spectacular at Radio City Music Hall. But that's it.)

I remember throwing up my hands and declaring to Rabbi Jason that I basically hated the whole furious frenzy.

He gave me a wry smile and said quietly, "I can give you a good reason to love December 25."

I couldn't imagine such a reason. "Please!" I pleaded.

For the next three hours, I listened as the good rabbi unpacked the secret of this biblical story in a way that left me in awe. (He will share it later in this book.)

Throughout these chapters, I have asked Rabbi Jason to take us deeper into the Scriptures—the same ones we have read over and over through our lives without ever mining the treasures that lie beneath. This is Jason's extraordinary gift. Every time you think he's finished with his point, he flashes a smile and says, "But wait! There's more!" And there always is. So much more!

Rabbi Jason Sobel is a colorful, funny, delightful, brilliant, given-to-rapping Messianic Jew. That term *Messianic Jew* simply means he is a Jewish individual who believes that the Messiah, who was prophesied 353 times in the Old Testament, has already come into the world in the person of Jesus Christ. Simply put, Messianic Jews believe that Jesus was and is the Messiah (or "Anointed One").

By that definition, I, too, am a Messianic Jew. My father was a Jew, so I am Jewish by birth. And I believe the Messiah has not only already come, but He is going to come again, this time to reign in His kingdom in a new heaven and a new earth.

Jewish friends of mine have often teased me about my *chutzpah*, a Yiddish term I always took negatively to mean "a little pushy." So imagine my surprise when Rabbi Jason explained to me that it actually means "holy boldness." Much better!

I want to be bold in my witness for Jesus, but I also want to be sensitive to the Holy Spirit. It's so easy to completely turn off people whose hearts are not ready to hear the Word.

Rabbi Jason taught me that Jesus came to undo all that we lost in the garden of Eden. He came to undo the ten plagues Moses brought down in the first exodus from Egypt, because Jesus is the final exodus—becoming the one and only Doorway into heaven, the restored Garden that awaits believers.

Another thing Rabbi Jason taught me is that from the first letter to the last, the Bible points to Jesus. On the third day after the crucifixion, two of Jesus' disciples were discussing everything that had happened in Jerusalem during the Passover. Jesus appeared to them on the road to Emmaus and said: "'Did not the Messiah have to suffer these things and then enter his glory?' And beginning with Moses and all the Prophets, he explained to them what was said in all the Scriptures concerning himself" (Luke 24:26–27). Jesus' statement on the road to Emmaus is very similar to one made by the rabbis who state in the Talmud, "The prophets prophesied only of the days of the Messiah."[1]

All of Scripture is meant to point to the Messiah in some way. For example, as Rabbi Jason explained to me, the first letter of Genesis is the Hebrew letter *bet*, and the last word of the book of Revelation is the Hebrew word *amen*, which ends in the letter *nun*. The first and last letters of the Bible spell the Hebrew word *Ben*, which means "Son." From the very first to the very last letter, everything in the Bible points to the Son!

When the old and the new are connected in this way, we experience what the two disciples experienced on the road to Emmaus when they exclaimed, "Were not our hearts burning within us while he talked with us on the road and opened the Scriptures to us?" (Luke 24:32). This type of Emmaus experience can happen repeatedly as you discover the Jewish roots and foundations of the Scriptures.

Throughout *The Rock, the Road, and the Rabbi*, Jason will provide his own unique thoughts and insights into many of the places we visit, the Bible passages we examine, and the truths we discover. You'll see his contributions in a different font throughout the book.

So join us, won't you? Come to the land, to the Word, and to the wonder of Israel—and to the Scriptures through which they all come together.

Meet the Tour Guide: Ray Vander Laan

In April 2012, my husband, Frank, and I went to Israel together for the first time. To say he didn't want to go would be an understatement. He was dreading it, and this from a man who had traveled all over the world as an athlete and sportscaster! But our dear friends Emilie and Craig Wierda had told me about a man named Ray Vander Laan, who was considered one of the greatest Bible teachers in the world, and about a tour he was leading in Israel.

My heart was hungry for more truth, but Frank felt he already had all the truth he needed. He had become a Christian decades earlier as a young boy growing up in poverty during the Depression. His parents were Christians, and his father worked as an itinerant oilman in California and Texas. According to Frank's mother's Bible, they moved twenty-nine times before Frank went to high school in Bakersfield, California. Frank remembered eating dog food—and being grateful for it—when life was particularly harsh. But his family always found a church each time they came to a new town, and many times that church was all they had other than one another.

What Frank didn't realize until our trip to Israel is that he had a *religion* all his life, but he never had a *relationship* with the living God. Begrudgingly, he agreed to go to Israel with me because he knew how much it meant to me. This trip became the prototype for what we now call the Rock and Road Experience.

Frank and I arrived at Ben Gurion Airport in Tel Aviv at noon after a ten-hour flight from New York City. I think most of the people in our tour group thought we would head to our hotel in Jerusalem, relax for the rest of the day, and then begin our study of the Holy Land rested and refreshed the next morning. But that's because we did not yet know our leader, Ray Vander Laan. Oh, we'd read his bio. We knew he was a teacher of biblical studies from Holland, Michigan, and the founder of That the World May Know Ministries. We knew he had a master's degree from Westminster Theological Seminary and had attended Yeshiva University in New York City, as well as Jerusalem University, with a focus on Jewish studies. But what we didn't know was *why* he had gone to such extensive lengths to study the Bible.

We soon discovered that Ray was an extremely memorable individual. Do you remember Indiana Jones from *Raiders of the Lost Ark*? Well, I immediately dubbed our teacher "Michigan Ray"! He not only looked like Harrison Ford, he even dressed like him and wore an Indiana Jones–style hat straight out of the Paramount Studios wardrobe! But Ray's message was completely his own.

"The problem with the Bible," he explained on the first day of our study tour, "is that the Bible was written *by* Middle Easterners *for* Middle Easterners. But we try to understand it with a Western mind-set. We try to apply our own principles and our Western understanding to a culture that is completely foreign to us."

That made sense to me. Our foreign policy has tried to do the same thing with nation building in the Middle East, with disastrous results. The difference between the Eastern and Western mind-sets is apples and oranges. Or more accurately, hummus and hot dogs. Culturally and historically, the East and the West are worlds apart. So how do we bridge that chasm when it comes to learning Scripture?

"By understanding what the Word of God—the Bible—*really* says," Ray explained.

After our flight landed, we were instructed to gather our luggage, put on our hiking boots, and grab our Bibles. There would be no lounging by the pool that day!

Then came one of my favorite memories on the entire Israel tour. We climbed straight up a mountain for about an hour to reach Gezer, a once-thriving biblical city that is now in ruins. I remember eighty-two-year-old Frank looking at me without an ounce of humor and declaring, "I am on the first flight out of here tomorrow."

"I'm right behind you," I said, wondering why we had agreed to such a trip.

When all of us jet-lagged pilgrims finally made it to the top of the mountain, I noticed Michigan Ray wasn't even out of breath.

The view was stunning. "Look down there," Ray pointed, "down to where we started out. See that tiny white ribbon following alongside the Mediterranean Sea? That's the Via Maris, or 'The Road of the Sea.' It's an ancient trade route dating back thousands of years." It was a beautiful sight, and it set the stage perfectly for Ray's first teaching session.

"People always ask, *Why the Jews?* Out of all the nations, why did God choose this stubborn, brilliant, but rebellious people to bring His message of salvation to the world?"

Ray clasped his worn leather Bible for emphasis and pointed below.

"Whoever controlled *that* road controlled the world at that time," he explained to our group. "It would be like God choosing Wall Street or Hollywood today. But in Jesus' time, that road was the center of commerce in the Middle East. To the north were Syria, Lebanon, and Turkey; to the east was Mesopotamia; to the south were Egypt, Libya, and Ethiopia. And to the west? To the west was Caesar."

MORE FROM RABBI JASON

We often refer to Jews as the "chosen people" because God made the nation out of a chosen couple, Abraham and Sarah. Part of God's covenant with Abraham and his children was giving them the land of Israel. This begs the question: why did God choose that land?

As Kathie mentioned, Israel's geographic position is key, since it functions as a land bridge between Asia and Africa. But from a spiritual perspective, there is even more. I believe the land God promised Abraham has the same geographic boundaries as the garden of Eden. When they ate of the forbidden fruit, Adam and Eve compromised Paradise and brought sin into the world. But through Abraham, Sarah, and their seed (the Messiah), God will restore heaven to earth, unifying Abraham's biological children with those in the nations who place their faith in Jesus.

CHAPTER 1

THE BROOK OF ELAH

David and Goliath

*[May] God . . . give you the Spirit of wisdom and of revelation in
the knowledge of him, having the eyes of your hearts enlightened,
that you may know what is the hope to which he has called you.*

—EPHESIANS 1:17–18 ESV

The next day of our Israel tour, we traveled by bus and then foot
(uphill again!) to the Valley of Elah—the place where David
famously defeated Goliath. Nobody was grumbling anymore. Not
even Frank. We had learned a great truth the day before: the harder
the climb, the greater the blessing on the mountaintop.

When we finally reached the ridge where the Israelites had looked
out with terror across the valley to where the Philistines waited to
attack, the first thing that struck me was how completely unchanged

it is. There is nothing there but the imagination you bring with you. And as you recall the familiar story of David and Goliath recorded in 1 Samuel 17, you can truly envision the drama that took place there some three thousand years ago.

Ray has the extraordinary gift of enabling people to see a familiar story with new eyes.

He explained, "Many people think the miracle in the story is how David, a young shepherd boy, was able to defeat the giant, Goliath—the champion of the Philistines, Israel's enemy. But the truth is that any shepherd worth his salt already knew how to defeat his foes. Shepherds were trained from their earliest days to protect their flocks from any enemy, including lions and bears. The Scriptures tell us that David had already done this. In 1 Samuel 17:36, David tells King Saul that he 'has killed both the lion and the bear.'

"So while King Saul and the entire Israelite army cowered in fear for forty days, this young shepherd, who was probably between twelve and fourteen years old, spurned the king's offer of his own armor and instead reached into the Brook of Elah, picked up five smooth stones, placed them in his shepherd's pouch, and approached the giant without fear. David said to Goliath in 1 Samuel 17:45, 'You come against me with sword and spear and javelin, but I come against you in the name of the LORD Almighty, the God of the armies of Israel, whom you have defied.'"

Ray paused to let all of this sink in.

"The miracle of David and Goliath is that David had an intimate *relationship* with the living God!" he bellowed. "That's what makes a miracle!"

Then Ray instructed all of us to go down to the brook and pick up a stone. By now we had learned to do what he said without questioning him. I will never forget the look in Frank's eyes as this man who was in six Halls of Fame obediently reached down to pick up his stone, just as a young shepherd boy had done three thousand years ago.

Ray also picked up a stone from the brook. As he held the stone in his hand, he looked at each of us, as if to the core of our souls, and asked: "What is *your* stone? Where are you going to throw it?"

He literally "rocked" our world. Frank and I and everyone in the group were never the same again.

This experience lit a fire in my belly, and it satisfied a deep longing in Frank's soul. Though the rest of the trip was profoundly moving and illuminating, it was this truth he learned in the Valley of Elah—that religion is nothing without relationship—that gave Frank a strong sense of peace and purpose until the day he died. Finally, at the age of eighty-two, he had found his stone.

As I stood on the mountaintop of Elah, I was filled with a sense of overwhelming awe. I was thrilled to be hearing for the first time what the ancient text truly meant. Centuries ago, Jesus said, "You will know the truth, and the truth will set you free" (John 8:32).

And I was starting to feel free, indeed.

As Ray concluded the day's teaching, he called each of our names, one by one, and challenged us to throw our stone wherever the Lord has placed us. "That's why every one of us who are created in the image of the Creator is on this planet," Ray said. "We are supposed to partner with God to bring His *shalom* to the chaos of this world. Genesis 1:1–2 says, 'In the beginning God created the heavens and the earth, . . . and the Spirit of God was hovering over the waters.' Think of Genesis 1:2 like this: '*Shalom* hovered over the chaos.'"

Ray explained that the word *shalom* has been diluted through the centuries from its original meaning to now mean "peace." But according to Ray, *shalom* really means God's *perfection. Shalom* encompasses all the characteristics of God—His righteousness, His justice, His unfailing love, His forgiveness, His holiness, and yes, His peace as well. *Shalom* is everything that is inherent in the one God and everything He planned for those He created. The garden of Eden was perfect, and all of creation, including human beings, was perfect—because God was, and is, and shall forever be *perfect*.

"So," Ray repeated, "we are to bring God's *shalom* to the chaos of this world."

There it was: our purpose! This is what gives meaning to our lives—what drives our passion, what fuels our very soul, and what ultimately fulfills our personal destiny.

But as we would soon discover, Ray had only begun to shake our foundations.

Come . . . to the Brook of Elah!

MORE FROM RABBI JASON

WHY DID DAVID CHOOSE FIVE SMOOTH STONES?

Over a forty-day period, the Philistine giant Goliath mocked and demoralized the army of Israel. Even worse, he ridiculed the Lord. Goliath's actions exposed the fear and lack of faith in the hearts of King Saul and his soldiers. But then David came along, and he couldn't tolerate the way the Lord's name was being insulted. He couldn't stand idly by as the people cowered in fear before this pagan blasphemer, even if he was a giant skilled in war. David was provoked to act.

So David went to Saul and said he wanted to fight Goliath on behalf of the king and his people. Saul, for good reason, was hesitant to allow young David to fight, but he conceded. He offered David his armor, but David decided not to wear it because it was too big. Instead, he would use a slingshot and five smooth stones from the river. Sounds crazy, right?

What is the significance of David using five stones? To answer this question, we need to dig deeper to understand this story from a Jewish perspective.

The name Goliath comes from the Hebrew root *gimmel, lamed, hei*, which means "to expose, reveal, or exile." He revealed the fear and exposed the weakness in the Israelites and their army. If Goliath had been a professional wrestler, he could have been called the Banisher or the Exiler.

I believe the five stones are key to understanding the story of David and Goliath. The Hebrew language is alphanumeric. This means that numbers can be written with letters. For example, the number five in Hebrew is written with the letter *hei* (ה), which is the fifth letter of the Hebrew alphabet. According to some Jewish mystics, the letter *hei* is connected to the divine breath of God that releases His creative power and potential. This is alluded to in the Hebrew text of Genesis 2:4, which says, "These are the genealogical records of the heavens and the earth when they were created, at the time when ADONAI *Elohim* made land and sky" (TLV). The Hebrew word translated "created" is *bara*, which means "created out of nothing." In this verse, *bara* has the letter *hei* inserted into it, which is grammatically incorrect.

There is no good grammatical reason for this word to include the letter *hei* unless the text is trying to allude to some deeper truth. But what? Remember, the letter *hei* is often seen as the letter of the divine breath of God, which, along with the Word of God, is the means by which creation came to be: "By ADONAI's word were the heavens made, and all their host by the breath of His mouth" (Psalm 33:6 TLV). So the letter *hei* in the word translated "created" in Genesis 2:4 alludes to the divine breath releasing God's creative power.

This truth can also be seen in the life of Abraham and Sarah. God promised Abraham and Sarah that they would conceive a child, but years went by without their having a son. As a sign that they would bear children even in their old age, that the promise would be fulfilled, the Lord changed their names:

> For My part, because My covenant is with you, you will be the father of a multitude of nations. No longer will your name be Abram, but your name will be Abraham, because I make you the father of a multitude of nations. . . . As for Sarai your wife, you shall not call her by the name Sarai. Rather, Sarah is her name. And I will bless her, and moreover, I will give you a son from her. I will bless her and she will give rise to nations. Kings of the peoples will come from her. (Genesis 17:4–5, 15–16 TLV)

The Lord changed Abram's name to AbraHam, and Sarai's to SaraH. There is a one-letter difference between their new names and their old ones—the addition of the letter *hei*, or H in English. The Lord added this letter to their names because it represented His creative power to accomplish the impossible!

Now it should make more sense why David picked up five stones. David needed the supernatural power that comes with the divine breath in order to punish Goliath, the wicked blasphemer, to restore honor to the divine name, and to bring *shalom* to the chaos. This is what the letter *hei*—the fifth letter of the Hebrew alphabet and the number five—represents in Hebraic thought.

In other words, David needed the *hei*, the divine empowerment of God's Spirit, to obtain victory and overcome the impossible!

The way to overcome the impossible has always been the same. Don't fear the giants. The Lord is with you always. Just believe and fight! You already have the victory.

CHAPTER 2

EN GEDI

David's Waterfall

*Let the one who hears say, "Come!" Let the one
who is thirsty come; and let the one who wishes
take the free gift of the water of life.*

—REVELATION 22:17

One of my favorite places in Israel is En Gedi. This oasis in the desert, directly west of the Dead Sea, is a steep climb dotted with ancient caves where young David hid from his enemy, King Saul, for years and cried out to God in dozens of profound psalms. All David's poetry about strongholds, hiding places, refuge, rocks, and living waters come alive here. We can only wonder what was going through David's mind during his time in the wilderness.

Perhaps David thought of Abraham, who was promised that he

would have a child, only to have to wait and trust for decades for that promise to come true when he was one hundred years old. David had been anointed king of Israel by the prophet Samuel when he was a young boy, only to wait until he was thirty to finally sit on the throne of the kingdom of Israel.

Haven't we all experienced excruciating times of waiting for God to answer our prayers? But the wait isn't idle time; the waiting period is our opportunity to be active and alive and growing, which is why it is so important that we persevere. As Isaiah 40:31 reminds us: "Those who hope in the LORD will renew their strength. They will soar on wings like eagles; they will run and not grow weary, they will walk and not be faint."

God's promise about the waiting time is as big a part of His plan as the actual moment when God's promise comes true. I doubt we are ever the same person when the promise is fulfilled that we were when the promise was made.

Although the landscape is bleak and the land is parched and dry, an amazing thing happens the higher you climb in En Gedi. Life begins to bloom all around you, wildlife bounds effortlessly on the heights, and suddenly, unexpectedly, streams and waterfalls of living water appear as if from nowhere.

The most famous of these waterfalls is the extraordinary David's Waterfall.

You catch your breath when you come upon it, and you can easily imagine how David and his men were overjoyed and praised God when their parched tongues tasted the water flowing from it and their weary, sun-scorched bodies stood beneath its blessed refreshment. You will never read the Psalms the same way after experiencing En

Gedi. The realization of God's unfailing love and faithfulness overwhelms you, and you weep tears of gratitude and praise.

Ray explained that the Judean mountains are made of limestone, so they are porous in nature, not rock-solid like granite or marble. "There—directly north, some seventeen miles from here—lies the town of Bethlehem. It's conceivable that the rain that fell in Bethlehem two thousand years ago in the time of Jesus is the very water falling over us here in En Gedi right now."

Imagine waiting two thousand years for living water! There have been times in my life, I confess, when I felt as if I was waiting that long for God's promises to be filled. Yet His timing is always perfect.

Come . . . to En Gedi!

LEAD ME, GENTLE SHEPHERD

(Inspired by En Gedi)

Lead me to the rock that is higher than I.
Hide me 'neath Your wings as You lift me through the sky.
Give me living water that I may thirst no more,
And when I go through storms, my Lord, lead me safely to the
  shore.

Chorus:
O lead me, Gentle Shepherd,
Let me hear Your tender voice.
And when we reach the crossroads,

Guide me toward the better choice.
Spirit, give me wisdom, show me Your sweet shalom.
Then lead me on to glory, Lord,
Lead me on to home.

Let me know Your truth, that I may understand
That nothing is created except by Your command.
In You I have my being, You give me every breath.
And You, and You alone, my Lord, have conquered even death.

Repeat Chorus

Tag:
One day the clouds will open
And all will see Your face,
And bow before Your lordship,
And praise You for Your grace.
And we will raise our voices in glorious harmony
And reign with You forever for all eternity.

—LYRICS BY KATHIE LEE GIFFORD

CHAPTER 3

THE JUDEAN WILDERNESS

Psalm 23

*Surely your goodness and love will follow me
all the days of my life,
and I will dwell in the house of the LORD
forever.*

—PSALM 23:6

While our tour group was in the wilderness of En Gedi, Ray Vander Laan reminded us of another well-known Bible passage that was likely written while David was in the wilderness: Psalm 23.

Most of us are familiar with this psalm, perhaps the most famous of all the psalms. On the surface, Psalm 23 seems almost like poetry, setting a beautiful, bucolic scene of the peaceful relationship between a shepherd and his flock. But as Ray explained, it is so much deeper than that.

The first line, "The LORD is my shepherd," is obvious. There is only one leader of a flock of sheep. And in Jesus, we have a benevolent, tender, and protective Shepherd who knows His sheep—and His sheep know Him.

Jesus said, "My sheep listen to my voice; I know them, and they follow me" (John 10:27). They follow Him because they *trust* Him. He has never let them down. Sheep can't see very well, but they have a heightened sense of hearing. They follow the shepherd's voice.

The next line in Psalm 23 is interesting: "I shall not want" (v. 1 NKJV). Perhaps a better translation is, "I have everything that I need because of Him."

The shepherd provides everything the sheep needs, even leaving the flock to go looking for the one lost member who might be in danger.

The next line is, "He makes me to lie down in green pastures" (v. 2 NKJV).

The truth is, there were no green pastures in Israel at that time— not in the way we think of rolling, grassy, lush fields. There were only small patches of grass in the Judean wilderness, barely visible except late in the day when the setting sun caused them to reflect light.

Ray explained that the shepherd's job was to lead his sheep to these life-giving spots so that they would be given exactly what they needed for that day. No more. This kept them in a constant state of trusting.

"He leads me in the paths of righteousness" (v. 3 NKJV).

"Paths of righteousness" are what the Hebrews called the ancient, well-worn paths that are still clearly visible winding through the hillsides today. Shepherds have used these same routes for centuries.

The Twenty-Third Psalm is a beautiful example of God's provision for each of us. He promises He will take care of us. He expects us to trust Him, and He gives us just what we need when we need it. In other words, "we live by faith, not by sight" (2 Corinthians 5:7). This is what leads to the eventual restoration of our souls.

Thinking about that restoration reminds me of a vivid memory from my precious father's last days. He was home under hospice care, and day after day my mom, my sister Michie, my brother Dave, and I sang hymns and prayed over him, holding him and whispering our love. One day we recited Psalm 23 over him. Finally, as my mother spoke the words, "Your rod and Your staff, they comfort me" (v. 4 NKJV), Daddy suddenly sat up, took a deep breath, and passed into eternity.

I believe with all my heart that Daddy went directly into the waiting, loving arms of his Shepherd, and it gives me great peace to know the truth of 2 Corinthians 5:8: "To be absent from the body [is] to be at home with the Lord" (NASB).

The rest of Psalm 23 is about the abundant, victorious life God promises to all His "sheep" if we continue to listen to His voice and follow in His footsteps.

Come . . . to the Judean wilderness!

CHAPTER 4

MOUNT CARMEL

Elijah and the Prophets of Baal

*"How long will you waver between two opinions? If the LORD
is God, follow him; but if Baal is God, follow him."*

—1 KINGS 18:21

The Old Testament book of 1 Kings records a dramatic showdown between the God of Israel and the false god Baal. At this
time, Israel had experienced a civil war and was divided into two
kingdoms. The Northern Kingdom maintained the name Israel,
and the Southern Kingdom was called Judah. The people of Israel
had largely abandoned the God of Abraham, Isaac, and Jacob. They
had been seduced by the false god Baal, who was worshiped by the
people who were not driven out of the Promised Land as God had
commanded.

The ultimate test of "Which is the greater God?" took place at the summit of Mount Carmel during the reign of the evil king Ahab and his even more evil queen, Jezebel. The prophet Elijah suggested that the followers of Israel's God (known as Yahweh) and the followers of Baal meet and "test" which was the one, true God.

In 1 Kings 18, we learn that King Ahab and Queen Jezebel had led Israel into unprecedented evil by worshiping pagan gods. Jezebel was from Phoenicia, and she was a priestess in the Baal cult. When she came to Israel, she set up a whole cult center to Baal that included 450 priests and 400 priestesses to Baal and Baal's consort, Asherah.

Baal is the pagan word for "Lord," and there were many different kinds of Baals in the pagan world, such as the "wisdom" Baal, the "military" Baal, the "health and wealth" Baal, etc.

But the supreme Baal was the "rain" Baal. This Baal was the god of fertility, who controlled the weather and provided rain. He was considered the god of the thunderstorm, and he was depicted as having lightning in his hands.

It was believed that this Baal would go into hibernation in the underworld during the summer season, causing the rain to stop. When fall came, Baal returned to earth to have sex with his consort, Asherah, thus bringing forth the rain again.

Today we understand they were in essence saying the rain symbolized Baal's sperm and the earth symbolized Asherah's womb. So, in order to get the gods to fertilize the land, the pagan believers mimicked these gods with their so-called worship. They would come to one of the Baal worship centers, marked by Asherah poles, and have sex with one of the priests or priestesses in hopes of enticing Baal and Asherah to mate. These centers were essentially houses of prostitution. Obviously, these pagan religious practices were completely contrary to the laws passed down to the Hebrews by Moses.

In times of severe drought or crisis, as they became more desperate, the Baal followers even sacrificed their children, either their own or the firstborn of a clan or family, in an attempt to win Baal's favor. In recent excavations near the capital city of Samaria, ruins have been found of a Baal temple built by King Ahab. Among the temple ruins were jars that contained the remains of infants and children who had been sacrificed in that evil place.

We can imagine what was happening during the years of drought described in 1 Kings 17. The people were starving, which caused them to become desperate, leading to sexual immorality and infanticide. This sets the stage for the great showdown between King Ahab and his false god, Baal, and the prophet Elijah and his God, Yahweh. Which of them would be the true "storm" God and send the saving rain? It was one of the most dramatic confrontations in the entire Bible.

The showdown took place at Mount Carmel, which means "the vineyard of God"—a reminder of what Israel was called to be for the world. But the people had forgotten the one, true God, and they had forgotten why the Lord had given them the land in the first place—so they would be a light to the nations, a kingdom of priests, declaring Yahweh to a seeking, hurting, and lost world.

The mountaintop was packed with people who still worshiped Yahweh, still said their prayers, and still sang their songs. But they had added the worship of Baal alongside their worship of Yahweh, making the pagan Baal equal to the Lord of all creation! This was the blasphemy that enraged the sovereign God. During the showdown on Mount Carmel, God sent down fire from heaven and proved to all who were present that He alone is God.

I believe it is this same kind of blasphemy today that breaks God's heart when we add false gods to our own worship. What have we allowed in our own lives to be equally or even more important to us than God?

The day our tour group visited this site—April 26, 2012—happened to be Israel's Independence Day (*Yom Ha'atzmaut*), commemorating the Israeli declaration of independence in 1948. Ray had just finished recounting the extraordinary victory of the God of Israel over Baal, when, just at that moment, sirens wailed below in the Valley of Jezreel. Then Israeli fighter planes emerged from the hidden silos beneath the ground and screeched through the skies directly above us. It was exhilarating beyond description. Even now as I write these words, my soul leaps at the memory of it.

God is still winning the victory. He is still fulfilling His promises. He is still sovereign over all things and all nations. There is a God in Israel! And He still loves His people and the land they were called to.

Come . . . to Mount Carmel!

CHAPTER 5

Caesarea and Herodium

Herod the Great

When King Herod heard this he was disturbed,
and all Jerusalem with him.

—Matthew 2:3

Other than Jesus, there is perhaps no biblical character more fascinating than Herod the Great. If Jesus is the greatest story ever told, then I believe Herod is the greatest story *never* told.

While there are a number of people named Herod in the Scriptures, we read about Herod the Great only in a couple of places—first as the king the wise men visited when they were seeking the place where the Messiah was to be born (Matthew 2:1–12), and then later when an enraged Herod sent his soldiers to Bethlehem to kill every male child under the age of two years old in the hopes of destroying any future threat to his throne and kingdom (Matthew 2:16).

But according to the historian Josephus and other chroniclers of the era, Herod the Great, who was born around 73 BC, lived a life of extraordinarily ruthless ambition, unbounded intellect, viciousness, and architectural genius.

Herod murdered the father of his favorite wife, Mariamne. He also drowned her brother and then murdered her as well, claiming she had committed adultery. He executed his most trusted friend, his barber, and three hundred military leaders in one day. He also killed three of his sons, suspecting them of treason. Finally, at the end of his life, he locked up three thousand of the leading citizens of Israel with orders that they be executed at the hour he died, to assure there would be sorrow and mourning on that day. Josephus wrote that Herod "put such abuses upon [the Jews] as a wild beast would not have put on them, if he had power given him to rule."[1]

Looming just a short distance away from Bethlehem is one of Herod's eleven palaces, Herodium, which Herod selected as the place where he would be entombed.

Herod was the governor of Galilee (appointed by Marc Antony) when in 40 BC the Parthian Empire conquered Judea and named a new king. Herod was more shrewd than loyal. He declared allegiance to Rome and fled Jerusalem with as many as five thousand people, including his family, under cover of night. Josephus wrote that, while fleeing, his mother's chariot overturned and trapped her underneath. When she miraculously emerged unscathed, Herod declared his gratitude to the gods and decided to one day be buried at that very site.[2]

For two thousand years, experts insisted that Herod's tomb was not in Herodium. But then in 2007, Herod's burial place was finally discovered by Ehud Netzer of Hebrew University, just where Josephus had written it was.

It is fascinating to climb down the cistern at Herodium and see where the earth has been packed and pushed forward to raise the height of the mountain. (One can only imagine how many slaves died to accomplish this.) Why would Herod go to so much trouble to raise the mountain? Because there was another mountain the same size next to it, and Herod, being the narcissist he was, demanded that his palace or burial site be higher than the one next door.

All of Herod's magnificent palaces were one day's journey from each other—from the north to the farthest south, to Masada, in the Dead Sea region. These palaces were, in essence, his escape route should things go wrong with the Jews or, even more dangerously, with Caesar.

Herod the Great needed Caesar because he needed Caesar's army, but Caesar needed Herod for a reason that has been lost to history. This is perhaps the most fascinating aspect of Herod's story.

Caesarea Maritima (also called Caesarea by the Sea) is an extraordinarily beautiful city on the coast of the Mediterranean, best known in the Bible as the place where Herod Antipas, the son of Herod the Great, imprisoned the apostle Paul. When you visit this city, you will see a plaque that mentions Pontius Pilate. We can assume Pilate was one of the thousands of soldiers who sailed to Israel on Caesar's ships to this man-made harbor at Caesarea. Only recently have experts finally discovered how King Herod was capable of going 120 feet into the Mediterranean Sea to pour concrete more than two thousand years ago. Why did he go to such trouble? If Caesar's ships arrived carrying soldiers, then what did they return with? The answer is surprising: King Herod and his family had a product that Caesar desperately wanted and desperately needed—the ancient version of Viagra.

It's important to understand the historical context. The Jews were the first monotheistic culture in history. They believed in one God and one God only. The Greco-Roman world of Herod's day was polytheistic. They believed in many gods, and much of their worship was sexual in nature. To facilitate this "worship," Herod had a product made from a substance extracted from the balsam tree, among other ingredients, that functioned as an aphrodisiac! Whether it actually worked, no one knows; but we do know from Josephus's historical writings that Caesar had a voracious appetite for this product, and he kept his ships coming and going between Capri, where he spent most of his time, and Caesarea Maritima on Israel's west coast, where Herod and his family made sure Caesar's ships were filled to capacity with their valued product.[3]

One of my favorite memories of Caesarea was when our group toured the ancient hippodrome, or athletic arena. Frank jumped up on a huge rock and immediately went into "sportscaster mode," holding an imaginary microphone to his mouth and saying, "Good evening, ladies and gentlemen, and welcome! This arena is rocking!" I don't recall his exact words, but I remember so well the joy in Frank's voice as he stood there in the arena. On our first trip to Israel with Ray Vander Laan in 2012, we visited the palace of Herodium, and I have a vivid memory of Ray teaching us the story of the Jewish Zealots' revolt against Rome in AD 70. The Zealots fled to the high spots in Israel in order to hold off the Roman assault. The most famous of these mountaintop fortresses is Masada next to the Dead Sea (see "Masada" on page 166). But they also went to Herodium.

Ray told us that when the Zealots broke into Herod's tomb, they discovered the sarcophagus, or box, that held Herod's remains. Archaeologists believe the Zealots smashed the box into six thousand pieces and blew Herod's ashes into the wind. This is symbolic of how despised Herod still was to the Jews seven decades after his death.

We were sitting in the area of the ancient synagogue on top of the palace when Ray recounted the story. Suddenly he threw his hat onto the ground and yelled, "Herod!" His voice echoed. *Herod! Herod!*

"Was it worth it?" *Worth it? Worth it?*

"Would you do it all again?" *Again? Again?*

The words of Mark 8:36 came to my mind: "For what will it profit a man if he gains the whole world, and loses his own soul?" (NKJV).

Herod had everything—a kingdom, a family, a thriving business, and a brilliant, creative mind. Yet he used all these things selfishly, narcissistically, and cruelly to build a monument to himself at the expense of everything and everyone else. He eventually died at his palace in Jericho, roaming the palace and murmuring, "Mariamne, Mariamne." He had lost his brilliant mind and his body wasted away. Josephus tells us that he stank so badly, even his servants hated to come near him.[4]

Every day as I read the newspapers, I see evidence that nothing has changed throughout the centuries.

Only what we build for God's kingdom will last. Nothing else is worth it.

Come . . . to Caesarea and Herodium!

CHAPTER 6

BETHLEHEM

Church of the Nativity

But you, Bethlehem Ephrathah,
though you are small among the clans of Judah,
out of you will come for me
one who will be ruler over Israel,
whose origins are from of old,
from ancient times.

—MICAH 5:2

I was deeply disturbed when our tour group visited modern-day Bethlehem. Scripture tells us Bethlehem was the birthplace of Jesus, the Messiah, prophesied in Micah 5:2 sometime between 750 BC and 686 BC (seven hundred years before Jesus' birth): "But you, Bethlehem Ephrathah, though you are small among the clans of Judah, out of you will come for me one who will be ruler over Israel, whose origins are from of old, from ancient times."

Today, the city of Bethlehem is controlled by the Palestinian Authority, and it feels—as my daughter, Cassidy, described it—"darkly oppressive." There are military checkpoints as you enter and exit. It hardly feels joyful or anything like the way the shepherds would have experienced it two millennia ago, as a place of great rejoicing at the Savior's birth.

Come . . . to Bethlehem!

More from Rabbi Jason

The Significance of Bethlehem

Shortly after the birth of Jesus in Bethlehem, an angel of the Lord appeared to shepherds guarding their sheep at night and announced to them, "Today in the town of David a Savior has been born to you; he is the Messiah, the Lord" (Luke 2:11). And the sign given to them was that they would find "a baby wrapped in cloths and lying in a manger" (v. 12). Of all the possible signs that could have been given to these shepherds, why did the Lord choose a baby lying in a manger and wrapped in swaddling clothes? Why was this so significant?

To answer this question, we need to dig deeper and explore the Jewish context in which the New Testament was written. Good students of the Bible are like detectives who ask lots of questions of the text. The first question we need to ask is: *Who are these shepherds? Is there anything unique about them?*

I believe these were no ordinary shepherds. They were Levitical shepherds, trained and tasked with the responsibility of tending and guarding the flocks used for sacrifices in the temple in Jerusalem.

Next, we must ask, *What is so significant about the location in which they found Jesus?* When it was time for one of their flock to give birth, the shepherds would bring the sheep into one of the caves surrounding Bethlehem that were used for this purpose. These birthing caves were kept in a state of ritual purity since these lambs were destined to be used as sacrifices in the temple. In fact, many of the male lambs born around Bethlehem would be used for the Passover.[1]

Since there was no room in the local inn, Mary and Joseph used one of these caves around Bethlehem. Messiah was not born in a stable behind some Econo Lodge or Motel Six. He was born in one of the many caves used for birthing these sacrificial lambs, because He Himself would be the ultimate sacrificial Lamb.

Not only would the location of Jesus' birth be significant to these shepherds, but so would the fact that Jesus was swaddled in cloths.

These shepherds were responsible for making sure that the newborn lambs did not contract defects, for only animals without spot or blemish could be used as a sacrifice in the temple. Baby lambs are very clumsy when they are born, so many scholars believe that these shepherds would swaddle their newborn lambs in order to prevent these future sacrificial lambs from becoming blemished by injuring themselves on jagged parts of the cave.

Another key aspect of swaddling in ancient Israel was "salting" a newborn. After Jesus was born, Joseph would have washed and scrubbed Him with salt water. Practically, the salt killed any bacteria found on an infant's body. But there is a lot of spiritual symbolism in this act as well.

Salt was symbolic of friendship and loyalty in the ancient world; it was a sign of covenant, as in the phrase "a covenant of salt" (2 Chronicles 13:5; Leviticus 2:13; Numbers 18:19). A common expression to denote friendship in Middle Eastern culture is, "There is salt between us." A salt covenant is used to denote the eternal covenant of friendship and kingship that God made with David and his heirs: "Don't you know that the LORD, the God of Israel, has given the kingship of Israel to David and his descendants forever by a covenant of salt?" (2 Chronicles 13:5). Jesus was not only born in Bethlehem, which is the city of David, but He was also the promised Son of David, the Messiah and King who came to fulfill the Davidic covenant—God's promise that one of David's descendants would live on the throne forever—and to establish the new covenant spoken of in Jeremiah: "'The days are coming,' declares the LORD, 'when I will make a new covenant with the people of Israel and with the people of Judah'" (31:31).

Salt was also an indispensable part of every sacrifice offered in the temple, as we read in Leviticus: "You are to season with salt every sacrifice of your grain offering. You are never to allow the salt of the covenant of your God to be lacking from your grain offering. With all your sacrifices you must offer salt" (2:13 TLV).

Not only was Messiah born in the same location as the temple offering, but He was also washed in salt as part of the swaddling process, which points to His future sacrifice as the Passover Lamb of God who would take away the sins of the world and inaugurate the new covenant (Jeremiah 31:31).

Messiah came to make a covenant with us, and He was so committed to us that He chose to die in order establish it, demonstrating how seriously He takes His friendship with us! This is what John 15:13 alludes to: "Greater love has no one than this: to lay down one's life for one's friends." Messiah was "the Lamb who was slain from the creation of the world" (Revelation 13:8), so He needed to be salted as our true sacrifice to erase our sin and bring us into a covenant friendship with the Lord. Now, that's a true friend. Isn't it amazing? We must make sure we are valuing His friendship and taking full advantage of it.

Not only was the process of swaddling significant to the shepherds, but I believe the actual garments in which the baby Jesus was swaddled were meant to be a sign to them as well. Let's explore their deeper meaning.

One of the oldest symbols of the Jewish faith is the menorah, a seven-branched candelabrum used in the temple. The Kohanim, the Levitical priests, lit the menorah in the sanctuary every evening and then cleaned it out every morning, replacing the old wicks with new ones.

What were the wicks of the menorah made from? The priests' tunics. Any priestly garment that became so dirty to the point that its stains could not be washed out was no longer acceptable to be worn during priestly service. These unusable garments were not destroyed; instead, they were cut up, and the fabric was used for another holy purpose. The tunics of the ordinary priests were used to make wicks for the menorah that was to burn continually in the Holy Place in the temple.

This is speculation, but I believe Jesus' swaddling clothes could have been made from the torn priestly garments that would have been used to make the wicks of the menorah. But where would Joseph and Mary have gotten them? My guess is that Mary got these cloths from her cousin Elizabeth, who was married to the priest Zechariah. As soon as Mary entered the home of Elizabeth, who had miraculously conceived in her later years, the unborn baby in her womb leaped, filled with the Holy Spirit. Elizabeth cried out, "You are blessed among women, and blessed is the fruit of your womb. Who am I, that the mother of my Master should come to me? For even when I just heard the sound of your greeting in my ear, the unborn child leaped with joy in my womb. Blessed is she who trusted that there would be a fulfillment of those things spoken to her by ADONAI" (Luke 1:42–45 TLV).

So the shepherd priests, who encountered angels, went to a place where the lambs used for the sacrifices were born and swaddled. There, they saw the baby Jesus swaddled like a sacrificial Passover lamb in priestly garments that were used for the lighting of the menorah in the temple, which symbolized the eternal presence and promise of God! Now it should make more sense as to why a baby wrapped in swaddling clothes and lying in a manger would be such a significant sign to these shepherds, for it pointed to Jesus being both the Lamb of God and the Light of the World.

CHAPTER 7

NAZARETH

Jesus Was a What?

"Isn't this the carpenter? Isn't this Mary's son and the brother of James, Joseph, Judas and Simon?"

—MARK 6:3

Our tour group was gathered, as usual, on top of a mountain when Ray asked us a question: "How many of you know what Jesus and Joseph, his earthly father, did for a living before He began His ministry as a rabbi when He turned thirty?"

Every one of us answered, "He was a carpenter." Smug bunch we were, indeed.

Then Ray again rocked our world by replying, "Actually, no. Jesus wasn't a carpenter, although there is no doubt that he did work with wood at times, along with other items."

Now, at this point, I was wondering what I was doing on a mountaintop 5,710 miles away from home with a guy who obviously didn't even know the basics of the Bible—with ten days of the tour to go!

This was the moment my life changed.

Ray explained, "The word translated 'carpenter' in Matthew 13:55 and Mark 6:3 for how Joseph and Jesus made a living is the Greek word *tektōn*. It means 'builder.' You see, when the writers of the King James Version were translating the Greek into the English, they assumed, 'Oh, these guys were carpenters. Just like us.'

"The problem with that is that there were no trees that could be used for building in Israel at that time like there were in England. All the wood in Israel came from the cedars of Lebanon, which were cut down, made into rafts, and floated along the Via Maris—'The Road of the Sea'—adjacent to the Mediterranean. There, they were broken apart and taken to the various construction sites."

Ray paused for his point.

"You see, there were only rocks in Israel. This is an example of one of the many poor translations in the Bible."

And then Ray gave us a stunning insight.

"Jesus was not a carpenter. Jesus was a stone mason."

I was shaken to the depths of my soul. Suddenly everything made sense! I remembered several Bible verses that referred to stones and building with stones:

- "Let any one of you who is without sin be the first to throw a *stone* at her" (John 8:7).
- "On this *rock* I will build my church" (Matthew 16:18).

- "The *stone* the builders rejected has become the cornerstone" (Psalm 118:22).

Then I asked the most profound question I have ever asked a man of God. "Ray, if we are wrong about something as simple as this in the Bible, what else are we wrong about?"

Ray looked at me with a mischievous grin and a piercing light in his eyes. "Everything," he answered.

And that's when I fell in love all over again with the journey, especially after Rabbi Jason explained Ray's revelation about Jesus' profession.

Come . . . to Nazareth!

MORE FROM RABBI JASON

JESUS THE PROMISED MASTER CRAFTSMAN

The Greek word *tektōn* can be translated as "stone mason" or "architect." All these concepts are significant in reference to Jesus, since they connect back to Him as the architect of creation.

The first word of Genesis in Hebrew is *bereshit* (pronounced "ber-ee-sheet"), which is commonly translated as "in the beginning." But *bereshit* can also be translated as "through the firstborn," since the Hebrew letter *bet* is also the preposition "through," and *reshit* (pronounced "re-sheet") can mean "firstborn." So Genesis 1:1 can be translated, "Through the firstborn, God created the heavens and the earth." And who is God's Firstborn? It is Jesus. The New Testament tells us He was the "firstborn over all creation" (Colossians 1:15) and "the firstborn from the dead" (Revelation 1:5).

Jesus is the *Tektōn*, the Architect of all creation. This reading aligns perfectly with the apostle John's understanding of creation. In John 1:3, he states, "Through him all things were made; without him nothing was made that has been made."

But there is more. The word *tektōn* can also be translated as "craftsman." The fact that the New Testament calls Jesus a *tektōn* is amazing, since Israel's Messiah is seen as a "craftsman," based upon the rabbinic understanding of Zechariah 1:18–21, which says:

> Then I lifted up my eyes and behold, I saw four horns! I said to the angel speaking with me, "What are these?"
>
> He said to me, "These are the horns that have scattered Judah, Israel and Jerusalem."
>
> Then ADONAI showed me four craftsmen. I asked, "What are these coming to do?"
>
> He answered, "These are the horns that scattered Judah, so that no one could raise his head, but the craftsmen have come to frighten them, to cast down the horns of the nations that have lifted up their horn against the land of Judah to scatter it." (TLV)

Commenting upon the four craftsmen mentioned in Zechariah 2, the rabbis in Jewish tradition state: "Who are the four craftsmen? Messiah son of David, Messiah son of Joseph, Elijah, and the righteous [High] Priest, [who will serve in the messianic era]."[1]

Jesus is the messianic craftsman whom Zechariah spoke about. The mention of two Messiahs in this passage might seem confusing. But in Jewish thought, "Messiah son of Joseph" is the one who will suffer to redeem God's people, and "Messiah son of David" is the one who will defeat God's enemies to establish the messianic kingdom. So, while many Jews see these two roles being fulfilled by two separate individuals, the New Testament teaches that Jesus at His first coming came as Messiah son of Joseph, who suffered as the "Lamb of God, who takes away the sin of the world" (John 1:29), and at the Second Coming will reveal Himself as Messiah son of David, who will establish God's kingdom as the Lion of Judah. When these two aspects of Messiah—"lamb" and "lion"—have been fully realized in the world, then the promise of Isaiah 65:25 will be fulfilled:

"The wolf and the lamb will feed together.
The lion will eat straw like the ox,
but dust will be the serpent's food.
They will not hurt or destroy
in all My holy mountain," says ADONAI. (TLV)

Jesus is the promised master craftsman and architect of creation who brings order out of chaos and *shalom* to our lives in this world and in the world to come! You don't have to wait to begin to experience His peace until His kingdom comes—you can have it right now as He promised: "*Shalom* I leave you, My *shalom* I give to you; but not as the world gives! Do not let your heart be troubled or afraid" (John 14:27 TLV).

What sets humankind apart from all other creatures? Only we are made in the image of God (in Hebrew, *b'tzelem Elohim*). The word for "image" in Hebrew is *tzelem*. It is derived from the Hebrew word *tzel*, which means "shadow."[2] A shadow does not act independently but is a reflected image. Thus, to be made in God's image means to reflect the image of our Creator. How is this to be accomplished? In Jewish thought, it means that we are to imitate God in all His ways, or as Paul wrote in the New Testament, "Be imitators of me, just as I also am of Messiah" (1 Corinthians 11:1 TLV).

Bringing light out of darkness and order out of chaos was one of God's first actions as Creator. We are called to do the same—to bring order and *shalom* to the chaos of the world around us. When we imitate our Creator, we allow God's light to shine in the midst of the darkness, thereby displaying our good works to others so they might glorify our Father in heaven (Matthew 5:16). Living as image-bearers brings order and *shalom* to a broken world, infuses our lives with meaning, and reflects God's image to those around us.

God longs to show the world His goodness through the way we live. But unfortunately, His goodness and peace can't flourish in the midst of chaos. The Lord always brings order before He fully manifests His blessing of peace. For this reason, when we care for His creation by working with Him to bring order out of chaos, we show His goodness to the world. As Jesus taught, "Let your light shine before men so they may see your good works and glorify your Father in heaven" (Matthew 5:16 TLV).

CHAPTER 8

THE JUDEAN DESERT

The Temptation of Christ

*Jesus, full of the Holy Spirit, left the Jordan and
was led by the Spirit into the wilderness, where
for forty days he was tempted by the devil.*

—LUKE 4:1—2

Scripture tells us that after His baptism by John the Baptist, Jesus
left the Jordan River and went straight into the Judean desert,
where He was tempted by Satan for forty days.

Jesus, full of the Holy Spirit, left the Jordan and was led by the
Spirit into the wilderness, where for forty days he was tempted
by the devil. He ate nothing during those days, and at the end
of them he was hungry.

The devil said to him, "If you are the Son of God, tell this stone to become bread."

Jesus answered, "It is written: 'Man shall not live on bread alone.'"

The devil led him up to a high place and showed him in an instant all the kingdoms of the world. And he said to him, "I will give you all their authority and splendor; it has been given to me, and I can give it to anyone I want to. If you worship me, it will all be yours."

Jesus answered, "It is written: 'Worship the Lord your God and serve him only.'"

The devil led him to Jerusalem and had him stand on the highest point of the temple. "If you are the Son of God," he said, "throw yourself down from here. For it is written: 'He will command his angels concerning you to guard you carefully; they will lift you up in their hands, so that you will not strike your foot against a stone.'"

Jesus answered, "It is said: 'Do not put the Lord your God to the test.'"

When the devil had finished all this tempting, he left him until an opportune time. (Luke 4:1–13)

Even though I have been to the desert region before and I know what to expect, I am always stunned by the bleakness and harshness of this part of Israel. I can't imagine lasting one day in the unrelenting and suffocating heat and brutal terrain. It is the most unwelcoming landscape one can experience, yet this is where Jesus was determined to go to strengthen Himself before beginning His earthly ministry.

The desert is a metaphor for our darkest experiences in life. The desert either destroys you or prepares you to emerge stronger and more powerful than ever before. I think too often we try to escape the hard tests in our lives as quickly as possible because, let's be honest, no one loves to suffer.

But if we can at least be aware that there is a deep and abiding purpose for our trials, it can give us hope that our suffering is never in vain. James 1:2–4 says: "Consider it pure joy, my brothers and sisters, whenever you face trials of many kinds, because you know that the testing of your faith produces perseverance. Let perseverance finish its work so that you may be mature and complete, not lacking anything."

God can and does use *everything* for His great purpose. As Romans 8:28 tells us, "We know that in all things God works for the good of those who love him, who have been called according to his purpose."

In the Judean desert, Satan offered up his kingdoms and his riches and his power to Jesus—if He would only bow down to him. Jesus responded to each of Satan's temptations in the same way: by quoting Scripture. Over and over, Jesus responded to Satan's temptations by declaring, "It is written . . ."—and this is the way we, Jesus' followers, should respond as well.

Because of Jesus, we can respond to the temptations of Satan by saying:

- "Get behind me, Satan!" (Matthew 16:23).
- "I am more than a conqueror because of Jesus Christ who loves me" (paraphrase of Romans 8:37).
- "I am a child of God, I am the offspring of the King, and therefore I am an heir to His kingdom! And just like Jesus, I still have work to do."

Come . . . to the Judean desert!

CHAPTER 9

THE SEVEN STREAMS

Jesus Calls His Disciples

*As Jesus walked beside the Sea of Galilee, he saw
Simon and his brother Andrew casting a net into the
lake, for they were fishermen. "Come, follow me," Jesus
said, "and I will send you out to fish for people."*

—MARK 1:16–17

Much has been made of the story of Jesus calling His first
disciples to follow Him. It's an extraordinary picture of a
young, inexperienced rabbi, fresh from His testing in the Judean
wilderness and eager to start sharing His *good news* (the Greek word
translated as "gospel") with a hurting world.

The whole area of the Sea of Galilee is breathtakingly beautiful. When you visit today, you feel as though the entire landscape is

strangely unchanged. The town of Tiberius on the west coast of the sea is the only developed spot, with charming hotels, restaurants, and a boardwalk allowing tourists to buy a ticket for a boat ride out onto the famous lake where Jesus calmed the storm and walked on the water.

There are no high-rise office buildings or residential developments in this area, and you find yourself grateful that it is still unspoiled. It makes it so much easier to imagine this place two thousand years ago, where Scripture tells us many of the stories involving Jesus took place.

Near the newly discovered ancient synagogue in Magdala, sitting directly on the Sea of Galilee, is a small, beautiful Catholic chapel called the Church of Peter's Primacy. I love it because it is simple and not ornate in decoration. The chapel, built in 1933, includes the ruins of a fourth-century church that commemorates the traditional spot where it is believed that Jesus called His disciples.

Scripture records the event like this:

One day as Jesus was standing by the Lake of Gennesaret [Sea of Galilee], the people were crowding around him and listening to the word of God. He saw at the water's edge two boats, left there by the fishermen, who were washing their nets. He got into one of the boats, the one belonging to Simon, and asked him to put out a little from shore. Then he sat down and taught the people from the boat.

When he had finished speaking, he said to Simon, "Put out into deep water, and let down the nets for a catch."

Simon answered, "Master, we've worked hard all night and haven't caught anything. But because you say so, I will let down the nets."

When they had done so, they caught such a large number of fish that their nets began to break. So they signaled their partners in the other boat to come and help them, and they came and filled both boats so full that they began to sink.

When Simon Peter saw this, he fell at Jesus' knees and said, "Go away from me, Lord; I am a sinful man!" For he and all his companions were astonished at the catch of fish they had taken, and so were James and John, the sons of Zebedee, Simon's partners.

Then Jesus said to Simon, "Don't be afraid; from now on you will fish for people." So they pulled their boats up on shore, left everything and followed him. (Luke 5:1–11)

The reason scholars believe this to be the actual location where this account happened is strictly scientific. It is the only place around the entire lake that seven separate streams of fresh water flow into it. According to Rabbi Jason, the number seven in Hebrew symbolizes completeness and perfection. It is used 735 times in the Bible—54 times in the book of Revelation alone. The number derives much of its meaning from being tied directly to the creation of the world (seven days) and to the seven annual Holy Days in the Hebrew calendar (see "An Overview of God's Appointed Feasts" on page 142). And Jesus performed seven miracles on God's Sabbath (Matthew 12:9–14; Mark 1:21–26, 29–31; Luke 13:10–13; 14:1–4; John 5:1–9; 9:13–16).

It is believed that because of these seven strong streams, fish were attracted to this area of the lake; therefore, the fishermen were too. While it looks like a calm beach you might find anywhere, because it receives seven streams of living water beneath the surface, it was the optimal place for teacher to meet student, for rabbi to meet disciple, and for God Himself to meet mankind.

Come . . . to the Seven Streams!

More from Rabbi Jason

Peter's Catch of 153 Fish and Second Chances

In John 21, after the death and resurrection of Jesus, the disciples went fishing in the same area—or as some believe, the very same spot—where Peter and several other disciples were first commissioned by the Lord to become fishers of men (Matthew 4). This means Peter's recommissioning and the disciples' new season of ministry to the Lord commenced in the very same spot where it all began at Tagbah, on the shores of the Sea of Galilee.

After fishing all night, Peter and several of the disciples had caught nothing. How could these experienced fishermen catch absolutely nothing? I believe there is a clue found in the Hebrew word for "fish." In Hebrew, the word for "fish" shares the same root constants (*dalet, aleph, gimmel*) as the Hebrew term that denotes anxiety, worry, and fear. The disciples, especially Peter, were fishing from a place of worry, fear, and anxiety. Not only were they scared the authorities might do to them what they had done to Jesus, but they were probably concerned about their future. Though they had been Jesus' inner circle of disciples, they had fled and hidden in His greatest hour of need; only John had not left Him. Surely they felt they had failed the Lord and had questions about their roles as leaders. When we fish from a place of worry and fear, our nets will remain empty like the disciples' nets. We must follow and serve the Lord not by fear but by faith!

At dawn, Jesus, whose identity remained hidden from the disciples temporarily, asked if they had caught any fish. After the disciples said no, Jesus, still unrecognizable to them, told them, "Throw your net on the right side of the boat and you will find some" (John 21:6). There were so many fish in the net this second time that they were barely able to pull it in.

Describing this great catch, John tells us, "There were 153 fish, many of them big; but the net was not broken" (v. 11 TLV). The large catch of fish was meant to remind the disciples that they had nothing to fear. Jesus had and would always provide for them if they remained faithful in following His instructions.

But of course, there is more! Every detail in the Bible is there for a reason. God does not waste words. Often, deeper truth is found in the details. One of the interesting details in this passage is that the catch of fish totaled 153. What is this detail meant to communicate to us?

First, I think it connects us back to Peter himself—his restoration after having denied the Lord three times the night Jesus was arrested and brought to the high priest Caiaphas's house (Matthew 26:69–74). But it also connects us to Peter's recommissioning, which happens later in this chapter.

In Matthew 16:15, Jesus asked the disciples, "But who do you say I am?" Peter responded by saying, "You are the Messiah, the Son of the living God" (v. 16 TLV). Jesus said to Peter:

> "Blessed are you, Simon son of Jonah, because flesh and blood
> did not reveal this to you, but My Father who is in heaven! And
> I also tell you that you are Peter, and upon this rock I will build
> My community; and the gates of *Sheol* will not overpower it.
> I will give you the keys of the kingdom of heaven. Whatever
> you forbid on earth will have been forbidden in heaven and

what you permit on earth will have been permitted in heaven."
(vv. 17–19 TLV)

I believe that Peter's confession can at least loosely be connected to the number 153 on several levels. First, 153 is the numerical value of the phrase, "I am the LORD your God" (Isaiah 43:3), as in "For I am ADONAI [the Lord] your God, the Holy One of Israel, your Savior" (TLV). Thus, the number 153 in John 21 hearkens back to Peter's confession that Jesus is Lord, which was the foundational confession upon which the church was built.

The number 153 is also the value of *HaPesach*, which is the Passover lamb described in Exodus 12:21: "Go, select lambs for your families and slaughter the Passover lamb" (TLV). Thus, the number 153 connects Peter's confession with Jesus' subsequent prediction of His death and resurrection, which links His divine nature and death as the suffering servant Messiah who is "led like a lamb to the slaughter" (Isaiah 53:7).

There is another textual link that connects John 21 and Peter's confession in Matthew 16. There are only two places in the New Testament where Jesus called Peter "Simon son of Jonah": Matthew 16:17 and John 21:15 ("Son of Jonah" is found in some ancient Greek manuscripts, while others say "Son of John"; but I believe Jonah is the better reading based upon the context and connection with Matthew 16). This is no coincidence but is meant to connect these two passages. Peter acted like Jonah by denying the Lord and running away.

Even though Peter had acted like Jonah, the Lord wanted to communicate to Peter that he was forgiven. He wanted to let Peter know that he was still "the rock" whom the Lord would use to be the first to publicly proclaim the good news to Israel, as well as be the first to bring the gospel to the Gentiles, which would occur in Acts 10 when

Peter preached to the Roman centurion Cornelius and his family. On account of the Lord's graciousness, "the keys of the kingdom" would still be entrusted to Peter to open the gates of salvation to the Jews first and to the Gentiles as well (Romans 1:14).

One final meaning of the number 153: as I mentioned above, John 21 happens in the same location or right near the place that Jesus first called Peter and Andrew, his brother, to be His disciples by saying, "Follow Me, and I will make you fishers of men" (Matthew 4:19 TLV). According to Jerome, an early church father, there were 153 species of fish in the Sea of Galilee, which ties back to the disciples being fishers of men.[1] Like Peter and the disciples, every follower of Jesus is called to cast their nets by faith for the purpose of drawing people into the kingdom of God.

CHAPTER 10

CANA

Turning Water into Wine

*What Jesus did here in Cana of Galilee was the
first of the signs through which he revealed his
glory; and his disciples believed in him.*

—JOHN 2:11

Much has been made of the fact that Jesus performed His first miracle at a wedding in the Galilean village of Cana by turning six large stone pots of water into wine. And He didn't turn the water into just average wine—it was the best wine possible!

Wine is mentioned 235 times in the Bible, according to *Young's Analytical Concordance to the Bible*. Some instances are variations of the word, as in *winepress*, but it is impossible to ignore the consistent presence and significance of wine in the biblical world. Interestingly, compared to the hundreds of uses of *wine*, the words *drunk* or *drunkenness* or *drunken* appear only eighty-one times in the Bible.

In Genesis 14:18, we read that Melchizedek, the priest of the Most High God at Salem (the ancient name for Jerusalem), "brought out bread and wine" for Abram and his companions. Many scholars believe Melchizedek was a preincarnate manifestation of Jesus—meaning that Jesus Himself came to earth earlier than when He was physically born to the Virgin Mary. Others disagree, but what is not disputed is that a blessing of "an abundance of . . . wine" was prophesied as a heritage to the chosen people—the Jews—in Genesis 27:28.

In that passage, Isaac said to Jacob, "May God give you heaven's dew and earth's richness—an abundance of grain and new wine." The Hebrew word translated "wine" in this verse (*tirosh*) does not mean unfermented grape juice, as some have suggested, because *tirosh* is an intoxicant if used in excess. Israel has a very hot, desert-like climate and there was no refrigeration in biblical times, so it was impossible to maintain freshness for any length of time or to keep grape juice from fermenting.

Wine is the most common alcoholic beverage mentioned in the Scriptures. In some places, it is used in sacrificial or medicinal ways, such as when Paul suggested that Timothy "stop drinking only water, and use a little wine because of your stomach and your frequent illnesses" (1 Timothy 5:23).

The Bible says clearly in Psalm 104:14–15 that God gave wine to make men *glad*. Referring to the Lord's provision for His people, the psalmist said, "He makes . . . wine that gladdens human hearts."

Of course, the Bible does mention drunkenness, as in the story of Noah in Genesis 9:20–22 and Lot in Genesis 19:30–38. Jesus, in

Luke 21:34, told His followers not to get drunk. The apostle Paul exhorted in Ephesians 5:18, "Do not get drunk on wine." You cannot get drunk on grape juice, no matter how much you imbibe!

Finally, we must remember how Jesus used the cups of wine at the Last Supper (see "An Overview of God's Appointed Feasts" on page 142), and how we continue to remember His sacrifice on the cross each time we take communion (1 Corinthians 11:24).

When Jesus turned the water into wine in Cana, the six stone pots that contained the wine held twenty to thirty gallons each. This was no small miracle!

In the Bible, God had directed His people to make wine a part of their festivals throughout the year, celebrating God's bounty with gratitude and joy. This wedding in Cana was a celebration—and Jesus enhanced the celebration with His first public miracle.

Come . . . to Cana!

MORE FROM RABBI JASON

JESUS' FIRST MIRACLE AND THE SIX STONE POTS

As Kathie indicated, Jesus' first miracle involved six stone pots of water that He turned into wine. Every word in the Bible is there for a reason, so what is significant about the number six?

The first thing we need to understand is that in numerology, six is the number of creation. The Bible tells us the Lord created the world in six days. Genesis 1:1, the first verse of the Bible, contains six words in Hebrew. The sixth day of creation is the day God made the first man and woman, the crowning culmination of all creation. And not only was man created on the sixth day, but in Jewish thought, Adam and Eve sinned on the sixth day, which is Friday on the biblical calendar.

But there is something even deeper about the number six that we need to understand. As I mentioned previously, the Hebrew language is alphanumeric, which means numbers are represented by letters. The number six in Hebrew is represented by the sixth letter in the Hebrew alphabet, *vav*. This is so important because *vav* is the letter used in Genesis as the conjunction that connects heaven and earth: "God created the heavens and [*vav*] earth."

In other words, the fall broke the *vav*, the connection between heaven and earth. So God in His goodness sent Jesus as the second Adam to reverse the curse in order to restore the connection between heaven and earth. Jesus died on the sixth day, a Friday, to make atonement for the sin of the first man and woman so the blessings we lost in Eden could be restored! Isn't it mind-blowing the way the Lord connects all of this?

Now it should make sense why the first miracle of turning the water into wine involved six stone pots that were filled to the brim. Jesus came to restore the Lord's original blessing for creation.

Jesus' first miracle is symbolic of what the Lord wants to do in you. Like the water into wine, God wants to transform you from ordinary to extraordinary. In Messiah you are a new creation: "the old has gone, the new is here!" (2 Corinthians 5:17). Ask God today to transform any emptiness in your life into fullness.

Jesus performed His miracle at a wedding in Cana of Galilee. But of all the miracles Jesus could have performed, why was His first recorded miracle turning water into wine? To answer this question, we must understand the apostle John's purpose for writing his gospel, which was to demonstrate that "Jesus is the Messiah, the Son of God" (John 20:31). The Messiah, according to the Torah and Jewish tradition, was going to be greater than Moses, as the Lord states in Deuteronomy 18:18: "I will raise up for them a prophet like you [Moses] from among their fellow Israelites, and I will put my words in his mouth. He will tell them everything I command him."

What was the first miracle Moses performed to demonstrate to Israel and Pharaoh that he was the redeemer sent by God to deliver them? He turned water into blood. But Jesus, the greater Moses, turned water into wine because He did not come to bring death, but so that we might have life and have it more abundantly (John 10:10).

Wine is one of the primary signs of the abundant blessings of the coming messianic kingdom. The messianic prophecy in Amos 9:13 states, "The mountains will drip sweet wine and all the hills will melt over" (TLV); the one in Isaiah 25:6 says, "On this mountain, ADONAI-Tzva'ot will prepare a lavish banquet for all peoples—a banquet of aged wine—of rich food, of choice marrow, of aged wine well refined" (TLV). By turning the water into wine, Jesus demonstrated that He was the promised prophet, the greater Moses, who came that we might begin to experience the abundant life of the messianic kingdom here and now through faith in Messiah Jesus.

It is also significant that Jesus performed the miracle of turning water into wine "on the third day" of the week (John 2:1). If there is a number or detail in the Scripture, it is there for a reason. The third day is one on which many traditional Jews get married, because it is the only day God blessed twice (Genesis 1:10, 12).

The third day is also connected to revelation. It was on the third day that the Lord descended on Mount Sinai and Moses led the people out of the camp to encounter the Lord (Exodus 19:16–17). Just as Moses and the Israelites experienced the revelation of God's glory on the third day, so Jesus revealed His glory on the third day.

The third day prophetically is one of redemption, restoration, and resurrection. Abraham offered his son Isaac on the third day (Genesis 22:4). And concerning the third day, the prophet Hosea declared: "Come, let us return to the LORD. He has torn us to pieces but he will heal us; he has injured us but he will bind up our wounds" (Hosea 6:1). Moses' first miracle on the third day was meant to point to Messiah's death and resurrection from the dead, which is the primary way Messiah makes known His glory to Israel and to the nations. By faith in Messiah, you can experience a third-day miracle by which you become a new creation, transformed from water into wine by the Lord's touch!

CHAPTER 11

CAPERNAUM

Headquarters of Jesus' Ministry

Leaving Nazareth, [Jesus] went and lived in Capernaum,
which was by the lake in the area of Zebulun and Naphtali.

—MATTHEW 4:13

Although Jesus grew up in the town of Nazareth, Scripture tells us He moved to Capernaum to establish a sort of headquarters for His earthly ministry (Matthew 4:13). This was strategic. Capernaum sits on the northwest coast of the Sea of Galilee. It was an important commercial stop along an ancient trade route.

This location of Capernaum was the first time our tour guide, "Michigan Ray," explained to us the use of parables in first-century Jewish life. Apparently Jewish men were not allowed to become rabbis, or teachers, until they were thirty years old. At that time, they would gather disciples and travel through the countryside speaking to the local people along the way and in the various synagogues on the Sabbath.

For centuries experts have debated the New Testament's claim in Matthew 4:23 that Jesus spoke in synagogues throughout Galilee, because they claimed there were no synagogues in Galilee at that time. They argued that the people simply went to Jerusalem and the temple for all the festivals and sacrificial offerings demanded by the law of Moses (see "An Overview of God's Appointed Feasts" on page 142).

But archaeologists have discovered the remains of ancient synagogues in Migdal, Capernaum, Herodium, Qumran, Masada, and most recently Magdala, where a synagogue was found eighteen inches below the ground. And in August 2016, *Kehila News Israel* announced the recent discovery of another synagogue at Tel Rechesh in lower Galilee, just four inches underground.[1]

I believe it is only a matter of time before even more sites are discovered, because historically the synagogue was central to the Jewish people and the Jewish faith. In fact, synagogues are still central to the Jewish faith—just as churches, temples, and mosques are equally important in modern society to the faiths they represent. They are the places where people of similar beliefs assemble to worship, celebrate, and pass on their traditions and faith to future generations.

The role of the rabbi in the Jewish faith is central to understanding the Jewish people. Rabbis were trained to be "good shepherds" to the common people who, like sheep, were simple-minded and in desperate need of leadership. The word *rabbi* means "teacher," and because most people in first-century Israel were uneducated in a formal sense, it was left to the rabbis to explain the fundamentals of the faith to the needy, seeking, often confused individuals who followed them on their travels through the countryside.

The rabbi would often begin by simply commanding, "Come!" and the people would follow and begin their journey with him. It was understood that the people were never to ask, "Where are we going?" or "What are you going to teach us when we get there?" If that sounds condescending, I assure you it was not. I am certain it was thrilling, not unlike taking a ride in an amusement park that promises thrills and chills, but you never know when they will come!

During our tour of Israel, Ray would begin each day with us all circled around him. Then we would recite the ancient Hebrew *Shema*, recorded in Deuteronomy 6:4: "Hear, O Israel, the LORD our God, the LORD is one." Jewish people have been reciting this verse every morning and evening since before the birth of Jesus. The Shema is the foundational Jewish prayer and their central declaration of faith. The purpose of reciting the Shema (which means "to hear") is to declare love and allegiance to the Lord, the God of Abraham, Isaac, and Jacob. It is also meant to testify to the world that God is One, that there are no other gods, and therefore we must serve and worship Him alone, even if this means laying down our lives. You can't imagine the beauty and power these words convey when you hear them in the land where they were first spoken.

After we recited the Shema, Ray—in an action meant to mimic these first-century rabbis—would thunder the command, "Come!" He would go up the mountain, and we would follow this mountain goat of a man at breakneck speed.

Rabbis in the first century were aware that the people who listened to them were uneducated, peasant folk for the most part. So

the rabbi typically spoke of things the average person could understand through their senses—what they could see or smell or hear or
touch or taste. Teaching in parables was an art form of communi-
cation at the most primal level, and nobody did it better than Jesus.

Out in a field, you could picture Jesus pointing and saying,
"Consider the lilies of the field, how they grow" (Matthew 6:28
NKJV). There are flowers everywhere in Israel. But instead of lilies as
we envision them, they are more like huge red poppies dominating
the landscape. They are just gorgeous!

At the time of Jesus, Capernaum was the "Millstone Capital
of the World." Even when you visit today, you will notice many
centuries-old millstones casually strewn about.

It's important to understand how crucial millstones were to the
economy and to the everyday life of Middle Easterners. Simply put,
a millstone is a pair of large, round stones used together in grist-
mills for grinding wheat or other grains. Think of it as an ancient
Cuisinart! The people's food supply depended largely on them.

Jesus said, "If anyone causes one of these little ones—those who
believe in me—to stumble, it would be better for them to have a
large millstone hung around their neck and to be drowned in the
depths of the sea" (Matthew 18:6).

I have no doubt that Jesus spoke these very words right there
in the heart of Capernaum, where the Sea of Galilee sits only yards
away. The people could not have missed His meaning. I'm sure they
loved the beauty and simplicity of Jesus' teachings just as we do
today, and they appreciated that He never spoke down to them or
belittled them as the Pharisees and Sadducees routinely did.

Jesus knew the longing in the people's hearts to understand the
truths He was teaching them. And He loved the purity of their

desire to know their Father more intimately. They needed hope, and Jesus delivered hope to them on a daily basis for the next three years.

Right next to the synagogue in Capernaum is an excavated site most archaeologists agree is the home of Peter's mother-in-law, not one hundred yards away from the synagogue. Scripture records that Jesus visited this home during His stay in Capernaum:

- "When Jesus came into Peter's house, he saw Peter's mother-in-law lying in bed with a fever" (Matthew 8:14).
- "As soon as they left the synagogue, they went with James and John to the home of Simon [Peter] and Andrew. Simon's mother-in-law was in bed with a fever, and they immediately told Jesus about her. So he went to her, took her hand and helped her up. The fever left her and she began to wait on them" (Mark 1:29–31).
- "Jesus left the synagogue and went to the home of Simon [Peter]. Now Simon's mother-in-law was suffering from a high fever, and they asked Jesus to help her. So he bent over her and rebuked the fever, and it left her. She got up at once and began to wait on them" (Luke 4:38–39).

I think it's fascinating that at this point in Scripture, only angels and women have served Jesus—the angels after His temptations in the wilderness (Matthew 4:11) and Peter's mother-in-law after He healed her. Later, we will hear of Mary (the sister of Lazarus and Martha) anointing Jesus with expensive perfume: "Mary took about a pint of pure nard, an expensive perfume; she poured it on Jesus' feet and wiped his feet with her hair. And the house was filled with the fragrance of the perfume" (John 12:3).

This was a demonstration of profound worship, and "life" always takes place just steps from where "worship" has been offered. Scripture says that God inhabits the praises of His people (Psalm 22:3). When we pray and we praise, we release the power of heaven to respond to our faith. Abraham was called a friend of God because of his faith, not because of his wealth or intelligence or strength or his standing in society. James 2:23 says, "The scripture was fulfilled that says, 'Abraham believed God, and it was credited to him as righteousness,' and he was called God's friend."

Millennia later, we continue to be called "God's friends" when we believe His promises to be true.

Come . . . to Capernaum!

MORE FROM RABBI JASON

JESUS, FORGIVENESS, AND 70 X 70

As Kathie explained above, Capernaum was the center of Jesus' ministry after He was run out of Nazareth (Luke 4:14–33). Capernaum is also the location where Jesus taught His disciples the true meaning of forgiveness. Peter asked Jesus: "'Lord, how often shall my brother sin against me, and I forgive him? Up to seven times?' Jesus said to him, 'I do not say to you, up to seven times, but up to seventy times seven'" (Matthew 18:21–22, NKJV).

Peter thought he was being very spiritual by being willing to forgive someone up to seven times. So Jesus' response—commanding him to forgive someone up to 490 times—must have been quite a shock! Everything Jesus did and said was very purposeful. He never wasted a word. So the number of times He instructs us to forgive must have some deeper significance. But what is it?

As we have already discussed, every word in Hebrew has a numerical value, and these values frequently communicate deeper spiritual insights. That is certainly the case here.

The number 490 is the numerical value of the biblical Hebrew word *tamim*, which means "complete," "perfect," or "finished." A person who can't forgive will always live an imperfect and incomplete life that lacks a true understanding of the "finished," gracious work of the cross. The number 490 is also the value of the Hebrew phrase "Let your heart be perfect" (1 Kings 8:61, my translation). Forgiving helps make us complete, and it is key to perfecting our hearts before the Lord.

But there are some even deeper connections. In Hebrew, the word for "my nativity" (*moladati*) and Bethlehem (*Beit Lechem*)—the city where Messiah was born, which means "House of Bread"—each individually adds up to 490. This makes perfect sense, since Jesus was born so that we might be forgiven. And forgiveness is associated with bread in the Lord's Prayer, which says: "Give us this day our daily bread. And forgive us our debts as we also have forgiven our debtors" (Matthew 6:11–12 TLV). Just like a person can't live without their daily bread, an individual can't survive without forgiveness.

The psalmist wrote, "If you, LORD, kept a record of sins, Lord, who could stand?" (Psalm 130:3). We need to learn to forgive and to be forgiven. How do we celebrate the forgiveness Messiah has brought us? By partaking of the broken bread of the Lord's Supper, concerning which Jesus said, "This is my body given for you; do this in remembrance of me" (Luke 22:19). Jesus, who is the Bread of Life, was born in Bethlehem, the House of Bread, so that we might both experience forgiveness and extend the bread of forgiveness to others. When we fail to forgive, it's like we are spiritually withholding food from a starving person!

Forgiveness is not an elective; it is a requirement for followers of

Jesus. We must forgive because we have been forgiven by the Lord. Extending forgiveness should not even be dependent on receiving an apology, as Paul wrote: "Bear with each other and forgive one another if any of you has a grievance against someone. Forgive as the Lord forgave you" (Colossians 3:13). For this reason, forgiveness is one of the greatest acts of faith and a true sign of faithfulness to the Lord. We must forgive because we have been forgiven. The practical benefit of forgiveness is that it frees us as well as the other person. Unforgiveness keeps you imprisoned and chained to your past, but forgiving is a key that sets you free.

Don't delay! Ask yourself as well as the Lord, "Whom do I need to forgive today?" Do you need to forgive yourself, a friend, or a family member? May the Lord give you the faith and grace right now to forgive in Jesus' name.

CHAPTER 12

THE SEA OF GALILEE

The Other Side

*That day when evening came, he said to his
disciples, "Let us go over to the other side."*

—MARK 4:35

One of the things that struck me the first time I visited the Sea
of Galilee was how few boats were out on the water and how
few buildings were along the magnificent coastline.

I asked Ray about this, and he laughed. "Well, historically, Jews
hate the water."

"What?" I exclaimed. "But it's gorgeous! And it's prime real
estate."

"Not to Jews. Think about it. All kinds of bad things happened
on water: Jonah was in the belly of a fish for three days. Noah and

the flood. Storms always came upon the Sea of Galilee. Jews are afraid of what the water represents—the chaos! The list is endless."

That is likely the reason that even the fishermen I observed around the Sea of Galilee stayed so close to shore when they fished.

I asked a friend who is involved in Israeli politics about the lack of development, and he explained that all the land surrounding the Sea of Galilee is owned by the government, so it's not available for purchase. But even if it were, it would probably be bought by non-Jews, who don't have negative views of the water.

Personally, I'm grateful that this pristine, magnificent landscape will likely never be developed. I imagine that today the Sea of Galilee looks very similar to what it must have been when Jesus walked along the shores.

Imagine how the disciples must have felt when Jesus told them to "go over to the other side of the lake" (Luke 8:22). Most of the disciples had spent their entire lives in the Galilee region. They had fished in the Sea of Galilee, even making their living as fishermen. They knew better than anyone the perils of this body of water. They knew that severe squalls could develop within minutes, with swells of waves up to twenty feet high. In other words, they knew a person could die out on that lake and never be found in the depths of the water (which is eighty-five feet at its deepest).

They also knew that on "the other side" were the pagan cities of the Decapolis—thriving, modern, vulgar, and forbidden by their Jewish law.

Yet here was Jesus, a righteous Jew, telling them to get in the boat and purposefully set out for the very place they had spent their entire lives avoiding. The disciples must have freaked out when

Jesus suggested this. This was unheard of! This was strictly forbidden! This was dangerous! And this was crazy!

They got in the boat anyway, and then look what happened:

So they got into a boat and set out. As they sailed, he fell asleep. A squall came down on the lake, so that the boat was being swamped, and they were in great danger.

The disciples went and woke him, saying, "Master, Master, we're going to drown!"

He got up and rebuked the wind and the raging waters; the storm subsided, and all was calm. "Where is your faith?" he asked his disciples.

In fear and amazement they asked one another, "Who is this? He commands even the winds and the water, and they obey him." (Luke 8:22–25)

Immediately they encountered a storm. I'm sure the disciples all thought, *See? I told you so.*

Jesus calmed the storm, but the worst was yet to come!

When they arrived at the shore, immediately a demon-possessed, naked, violent, bloody-from-cutting-himself man came screaming at them from the tombs! This man was the picture of death, except he wasn't dead. It had to be terrifying to the disciples.

But not to Jesus. Jesus was the only one who got out of the boat.

What I love about this story is the reason that Jesus got in the boat in the first place—to go over to the other side and save this one, pathetic, seemingly hopeless man!

Jesus came to bring His *shalom* to the chaos, to dress this man in a robe of righteousness, and ultimately to set him free! Free to go home to his family and his neighbors as a living testimony to God's mercy and forgiveness and redemption.

What boat does Jesus want us to get into?

Where does He want us to sail?

Whom does He want us to greet in love and mercy when they run screaming at us in their chaos?

Ray concluded his teaching of this story by reminding us that at the end of the gospel of Mark, we see Jesus exchanging places with this man on the cross. Now Jesus was the one who was naked, crying out, bloodied, and driven into the tomb. This is how we are made whole—Jesus exchanges His life for ours, His cleanness for our uncleanness.

He defeats evil by absorbing evil into Himself.

He brings His *shalom* to the chaos by taking on all the world's chaos so He can offer us true peace.

Come . . . to the Sea of Galilee!

CHAPTER 13

MAGDALA

Mary Magdalene and the Women Jesus Loved

*When Jesus rose early on the first day of the week, he appeared first
to Mary Magdalene, out of whom he had driven seven demons.*

—MARK 16:9

Mary Magdalene holds a very special place among the followers of Jesus. She was not like any typical disciple—in fact,
she lacked any relevance at all to the people of her day. She was
not a man, not a fisherman, not a tax collector. She was obviously
a woman—but no ordinary woman. Mary of Magdala, a village
recently discovered along the southern shores of the Sea of Galilee,
is mentioned twelve times in the Gospels, more than most of the
apostles.

Both the gospel of Mark and the gospel of Luke record that Jesus had cast seven demons out of Mary Magdalene at some point in His earthly ministry (Mark 16:9; Luke 8:2). The Bible tells us she was present at Jesus' crucifixion and was the first on the scene at His grave after the resurrection:

> Early on the first day of the week, while it was still dark, Mary Magdalene went to the tomb and saw that the stone had been removed from the entrance. So she came running to Simon Peter and the other disciple, the one Jesus loved, and said, "They have taken the Lord out of the tomb, and we don't know where they have put him!" (John 20:1–2)

I believe Jesus was the first and greatest feminist in history because of the value He placed on the women He met during His lifetime. Jesus overruled centuries of customs and traditions in the ancient world that often resulted in women being treated as second-class citizens. Just as importantly, Jesus actively elevated women above their normal status and role in both the secular culture of His day and in first-century Judaism.

For example, Jesus talked to the Samaritan woman, who was considered to be doubly unclean because she was not only female but also a foreigner. Yet look at Jesus' interaction with her: "When a Samaritan woman came to draw water, Jesus said to her, 'Will you give me a drink?'" (John 4:7).

I love the way Jesus saw into her heart. Instead of drawing water with the other women during the coolest hours of the morning or late afternoon, she was alone at the well at noon—a sure sign she was avoiding the other townspeople due to her terrible reputation.

Jesus told this Samaritan woman the truth about herself, but not in a condemning way. Instead, He treated her with respect and valued her in a way no man ever had, certainly none of her five previous husbands. Scripture says that after her encounter with Jesus, the Samaritan woman went back to her village and told the people all about Jesus—and they, in turn, went out to meet Him. Jesus made this downtrodden, much used, and tainted woman a star in her own community! Jesus never left anyone the same after an encounter with Him.

Jesus also called a woman who had been crippled a "daughter of Abraham," implying equal status with a man, or "son of Abraham." In Luke 13:16, He said, "Should not this woman, a daughter of Abraham, whom Satan has kept bound for eighteen long years, be set free on the Sabbath day from what bound her?" Calling a woman "a daughter of Abraham" was unparalleled in Scripture, and in fact, it occurs nowhere else in the Bible!

There is perhaps no greater evidence of the value Jesus placed on women than the fact that He welcomed them into His inner circle of devoted followers, with perhaps as many as half of His followers being female (including Mary Magdalene, Joanna, Susanna, and Mary and Martha, among others). Throughout the Bible, women had an important role in the leadership of God's people and their redemption.

In John 19:25–27, we see that Jesus loved and honored His mother, Mary, so much that even in His last hours, before His death on the cross, He was concerned for her welfare:

> Near the cross of Jesus stood his mother, his mother's sister, Mary
> the wife of Clopas, and Mary Magdalene. When Jesus saw his
> mother there, and the disciple whom he loved standing nearby,
> he said to her, "Woman, here is your son," and to the disciple,

"Here is your mother." From that time on, this disciple took her into his home.

As the firstborn son in a Jewish family, Jesus was held responsible for every member. But we read in John 7:5 that before His resurrection, "Even his own brothers did not believe in him," which meant that He couldn't leave His beloved mother in their care. So He chose to entrust the care of His mother instead to the apostle John.

After His resurrection, Jesus showed compassion to Mary Magdalene. In Mark 16:9, we read, "When Jesus rose early on the first day of the week, he appeared first to Mary Magdalene, out of whom he had driven seven demons." I love that in her grief and fear, Mary Magdalene didn't recognize Jesus until He tenderly said her name: "Jesus said to her, 'Mary.' She turned to him and cried out in Aramaic, 'Rabboni!' (which means 'Teacher')" (John 20:16). This reduces me to tears every time I think of it because I, too, experience grief, confusion, and fear. And the thought that Jesus might lovingly whisper my name—seeing me, knowing me, loving me—is as profound an experience as I can imagine. How tender! How revolutionary! Jesus is the radical lover of women!

It is difficult for us in our modern, Western culture to fathom a world where women were worth less than a camel, required to remove themselves from society during each menstrual cycle, forbidden to talk to any men outside of their family, or even to count change from their hands into the hands of a male. During that time, a husband could divorce his wife, but a wife had no legal option to leave her husband, no matter how abusive he might be. There are many more examples of the lower status women received in ancient Israel—and pretty much everywhere else in the civilized world.

But, for me, there is one story in Scripture that showcases Jesus' love and respect for women: the woman caught in adultery.

Come . . . to Magdala!

MORE FROM RABBI JASON

THE WOMAN CAUGHT IN ADULTERY AND WHY JESUS WROTE IN THE SAND

Yeshua went to the Mount of Olives. At dawn, He came again into the Temple. All the people were coming to Him, and He sat down and began to teach them.

The *Torah* scholars and Pharisees bring in a woman who had been caught in adultery. After putting her in the middle, they say to *Yeshua*, "Teacher, this woman has been caught in the act of committing adultery. In the *Torah*, Moses commanded us to stone such women. So what do You say?" Now they were saying this to trap Him, so that they would have grounds to accuse Him.

But *Yeshua* knelt down and started writing in the dirt with His finger. When they kept asking Him, He stood up and said, "The sinless one among you, let him be the first to throw a stone at her." Then He knelt down again and continued writing on the ground.

Now when they heard, they began to leave, one by one, the oldest ones first, until *Yeshua* was left alone with the woman in the middle. Straightening up, *Yeshua* said to her, "Woman, where are they? Did no one condemn you?"

"No one, Sir," she said.

"Then neither do I condemn you," *Yeshua* said. "Go, and sin no more." (John 8:1–11 TLV)

Some Torah scholars and Pharisees brought a woman who was caught in adultery to Jesus. They wanted to know Jesus' opinion as to the punishment this woman should face. They thought this question would trap Jesus, for if He said that they should stone her, then He would be viewed as cruel. But if He said that the adulterous woman should be forgiven and the law not followed, then He could be accused of violating the Torah and being too liberal. Jesus, who operated in the Spirit of wisdom, responded in a way that prevented them from entrapping Him but also demonstrated the heart of the Father. He turned the tables on these leaders when, after writing in the dirt, He said, "The sinless one among you, let him be the first to throw a stone at her" (John 8:7 TLV). That statement had a powerful effect on those who heard it. The accusers of the woman caught in adultery left one by one.

It seems from the text that Jesus' act of kneeling down and writing in the dirt also played a key part in causing the Torah scholars and Pharisees to leave without saying a word.

Why did Jesus do this, and what could He have written that would have had such a profound effect? There is no way to be certain, but there seem to be a few clues in the text. There are four key components to what Jesus did:

- Jesus used His finger to write.
- Jesus wrote with His finger twice.
- Jesus wrote specifically in the dirt, and
- Jesus knelt to write.

First, let's explore the first and second clues, Jesus' use of His finger and writing in the dirt twice.

After bringing the Israelites out of Egypt, the Lord brought them to Mount Sinai and gave them the Ten Commandments on two stone tablets that were "written by the finger of God" (Exodus 31:18 TLV). But as Moses was coming down Mount Sinai to give the people the two tablets, he saw them worshiping a golden calf. What did Moses do? He smashed the tablets that were "written by the finger of God" because he saw the people committing idolatry, which is a spiritual form of adultery in the Lord's eyes: "backsliding Israel committed adultery" (Jeremiah 3:8 TLV). It was fitting that Moses smashed the two tablets of testimony, because they symbolized in rabbinic thought the traditional Jewish wedding contract known as a *ketubah*, given to every bride on her wedding day.

God in His grace did not divorce Israel because of her spiritual adultery, but forgave her after Moses pled for forgiveness. After going up Sinai again, Moses came down with another set of tablets. This second set of tablets was a key sign that the Lord had forgiven Israel and was giving her a second chance. Moses descended with the second pair of tablets on the Day of Atonement, the holiest day of the year. On this day, Israel's high priest was commanded to enter into the Holy of Holies to sprinkle the blood of the special animal sacrifices on the mercy seat of the ark, in hopes that the Lord would accept his offering and forgive their sins (see "An Overview of God's Appointed Feasts" on page 142), which points to the Lord's grace and forgiveness.

When Jesus wrote in the dirt, it was just a few days after the Day of Atonement. Jesus' action of writing in the dirt reminded these leaders that they, too, were guilty of breaking the Ten Commandments and needed atonement, which they had just fasted and prayed for less than a week prior. And it was during this season of the Day of Atonement that the Lord had forgiven Israel, who had acted as an unfaithful wife by committing spiritual adultery through idolatrous actions.

If the Lord had forgiven Israel during this same season for a similar sin, then what right did the religious leaders have to condemn this woman? In summary, Jesus' writing in the dirt reminded the Pharisees and Sadducees of the Ten Commandments given by the finger of God, and His writing in the dirt twice reminded them that God had given Israel a second chance by giving them a second set of tablets. In light of this, who among them was worthy to cast the first stone?

The third aspect of this story that needs to be examined is why Jesus wrote in the dirt. I believe it was to remind these leaders where they came from. Man was created from the dirt (Genesis 2:7), and as such we are all weak and vulnerable to temptation. Jewish tradition says there was once a rabbi named Simcha Bunem who carried two slips of paper, one in each pocket. On one piece it was written, "For my sake the world was created" and on the other piece, "I am but dust and ashes." Every person has such worth that the world was created for them, but on the other hand, we need to be humble, for we come from the dirt and are all sinners who fall short of God's glory (Romans 3:23).

And finally, I love the fact that Jesus knelt to write. Think about it for a moment. Several influential men were standing around this woman, pointing accusatory fingers at her as she probably knelt down in fear and shame. What did Jesus do? He knelt as well, in part to get down on her level. He did not stand over her but got down in the dirt with her. This is such a beautiful picture of the love of Jesus! He meets us where we are and never looks down on us.

Jesus was clear that this woman should sin in this way no more. Yet even though she was guilty, Jesus didn't condemn her, but showed her grace and told her she was forgiven and free to go.

CHAPTER 14

GALILEE

The Woman Who Was Healed by a Touch

*[Jesus] said to her, "Daughter, your faith has healed
you. Go in peace and be freed from your suffering."*

—MARK 5:34

It's difficult in our modern culture to imagine what life was
like in Israel during the time of Jesus. The Jews experienced
terrible suffering under Roman rule—physically, emotionally, and
spiritually.

The Romans were brutal, violent oppressors who took every
opportunity to whip their subjects into submission. They despised
the Jewish faith and saw it as inferior to their polytheistic worldview.
The Jews, in return, despised the Romans because of their oppressive taxes and their "unclean" culture and pagan religion. And more

than anything, the Jews resented the Romans' absolute power over their daily life and worship.

Daily living for every Jew was an act of faith. They spent each waking moment trying to keep not only the Torah—the Mosaic law—but also the extra six-hundred-plus man-made laws imposed on them by the Pharisees and the Sadducees. We can't imagine the weight of such a legalistic burden on everyday life. No one could be pure enough, or holy enough, or without blemish before God under such self-righteous leaders.

The Pharisees and the Sadducees, however, took great pains to parade their intellectual and spiritual superiority before the people. Jesus saved His sternest words for these individuals. In Matthew 23:27, Jesus said: "Woe to you, teachers of the law and Pharisees, you hypocrites! You are like whitewashed tombs, which look beautiful on the outside but on the inside are full of the bones of the dead and everything unclean."

Jesus came to ease the burdens on the Jewish people. In Matthew 11:28–30, He said: "Come to me, all you who are weary and burdened, and I will give you rest. Take my yoke upon you and learn from me, for I am gentle and humble in heart, and you will find rest for your souls. For my yoke is easy and my burden is light."

No wonder the people's hearts soared when they heard Him teach! No one in their world ever spoke such words of life or hope or compassion to them. Such love! Jesus' words still have the same effect today on those whose hearts are open to His tender message of grace.

Perhaps no one in the ancient world longed for Jesus' message of grace more than the women in first-century Israel. As we mentioned in the previous chapter, it is important to understand the status of women in ancient times. Their freedoms were severely limited by the Jewish law and traditions. They were basically confined to their father's or their husband's home and had no authority of their own.

During this time women were considered inferior to men and weren't even allowed to testify in court trials, as they were not deemed to be credible witnesses. They were considered second-class citizens, excluded from worship among the men, with little more status than slaves.

But Jesus consistently demonstrated that He had a high respect and value for women.

One of my favorite stories of Jesus' love for women is in Mark 5, when He healed a woman whose menstrual cycle had caused her to suffer for twelve years. She touched the hem of His garment (a major violation of the law as a woman), and He broke the law as well by talking to her in public:

And a woman was there who had been subject to bleeding for twelve years. She had suffered a great deal under the care of many doctors and had spent all she had, yet instead of getting better she grew worse. When she heard about Jesus, she came up behind him in the crowd and touched his cloak, because she thought, "If I just touch his clothes, I will be healed." Immediately her bleeding stopped and she felt in her body that she was freed from her suffering.

At once Jesus realized that power had gone out from him. He turned around in the crowd and asked, "Who touched my clothes?"

"You see the people crowding against you," his disciples answered, "and yet you can ask, 'Who touched me?'"

But Jesus kept looking around to see who had done it. Then the woman, knowing what had happened to her, came and fell at his feet and, trembling with fear, told him the whole truth. He said to her, "Daughter, your faith has healed you. Go in peace and be freed from your suffering" (Mark 5:25–34).

Rabbi Jason has some beautiful insights about this story of Jesus' love for the woman with the issue of blood.

Come . . . to Galilee!

More from Rabbi Jason

Jesus and the Woman with the Issue of Blood

Yeshua got up and began to follow him, with His disciples.

Just then a woman, losing blood for twelve years, came from behind and touched the *tzitzit* of His garment. For she kept saying to herself, "If only I touch His garment, I will be healed."

But then *Yeshua* turned and saw her. "Take heart, daughter," He said, "your faith has made you well." That very hour the woman was healed. (Matthew 9:19–22 TLV)

A woman who had been suffering with bleeding for twelve years reached out and grabbed the hem of Jesus' garment. Jesus responded by saying, "Someone touched me; I know that power has gone out from me" (Luke 8:46). The woman, realizing that she could not hide, "came trembling and fell at his feet," telling Jesus why she had touched Him and how she had been healed instantly.

The bleeding woman had every reason to be fearful. Among religious

Jews, it was—and still is—considered immodest and inappropriate to touch a man, even one's husband, in public. But even worse, this woman was ritually unclean and could spread her impurity to any person she touched (Leviticus 15:25–27). She could have faced serious consequences for such a bold action.

But this woman was desperate. Imagine not being touched by family or friends for twelve years. She had lived for over a decade in a perpetual state of shame as an outcast who was excluded from the social and spiritual life of her community. She felt she had nothing to lose, so she took a big risk. When she touched the hem of Jesus' garment, she was instantly healed! Though Jesus became ritually unclean by her touch, she became clean, and more importantly, whole again.

Notice this woman's fear: "The woman, knowing what had happened to her, came and fell at his feet and, trembling with fear, told him the whole truth" (Mark 5:33). Notice also Jesus' gentle response: "Daughter, your faith has healed you. Go in peace" (v. 34). This underscores how radically differently Jesus dealt with women than did other men of His day. Rather than being upset with her, which would have been the normal reaction from a rabbi or Levitical priest, He commended the woman's faith.

But of course, there is something more! A key detail often overlooked in this passage is that the woman touched "the edge of his cloak" (Matthew 9:20). She did not just touch the fringe, but rather His *tzitzit*, the ritual tassels placed on each corner (*kanaf*, in Hebrew) of every four-corner garment. These *tzitzit* are described in the book of Numbers:

> Adonai spoke to Moses saying, "Speak to *Bnei-Yisrael.* Say to them that they are to make for themselves *tzitzit* on the corners

of their garments throughout their generations, and they are to put a blue cord on each *tzitzit*. It will be your own *tzitzit*—so whenever you look at them, you will remember all the *mitzvot* of ADONAI and do them and not go spying out after your own hearts and your own eyes, prostituting yourselves. This way you will remember and obey all My *mitzvot* and you will be holy to your God. I am ADONAI your God. I brought you out of the land of Egypt to be your God. I am ADONAI your God." (Numbers 15:37–41 TLV)

These *tzitzit* were meant to remind Israel to faithfully follow the Lord by obeying His commandments. It is no coincidence that they were to be placed on all four corners of the garment.

The root of all sin goes back to the garden of Eden. The result of Adam and Eve's disobedience was exile for them and all their descendants after them. Living in exile means living in a perpetual state of disconnection and separation that ultimately leads to death if not remedied. There are four aspects to exile: spiritual, emotional, relational, and physical.

The promise of redemption from exile is also connected to the number four. At the Passover Seder, there are four cups of wine that correspond to the four aspects of redemption mentioned in Exodus 6:6–7 (TLV): "I will bring you out," "I will deliver you," "I will redeem you," "I will take you to Myself" (see "An Overview of God's Appointed Feasts" on page 142). At the final redemption, the Lord will "lift up a banner for the nations, and assemble the dispersed of Israel, and gather the scattered of Judah from the four corners of the earth" (Isaiah 11:12 TLV).

Also, there is a messianic promise that states, "For you who revere

My Name, the sun of righteousness will rise, with healing in its wings" (Malachi 3:20 TLV). The word for "wings" in this verse literally means "corner" and is the same word used for the tassels on the four corners, known in Hebrew as the *arba kanfot*. This woman reached out and grabbed one of the four "wings" of Jesus' tunic.

This bleeding woman had been living in exile on all four levels. She had no physical contact with family and friends, could not publicly worship in the temple, was isolated and alone, and lived in a perpetual state of physical pain. But she found a fourfold healing by touching one of the four corners of Jesus' garment, and thus she became an example of the messianic redemption that we can begin to experience right now when we reach out and touch Him! Like her, we must have the faith to boldly reach out and seize the Lord so that we might find help and healing in our time of need.

Just like the woman with the issue of blood was viewed as unclean, many religious leaders in Jesus' day viewed the Gentile nations as unclean and unworthy. This perspective was due to the fact that the nations of the world were pagan at this time, and their cultures were dominated by idolatry, bloodshed, and sexual immorality. Despite this, Jesus had a very different view of Gentiles. He did not focus on their sin but on God's promise of redemption for all people.

Just like the woman who grabbed hold of Him and found personal redemption, one day all the nations of the world will do the same. As the prophet Zechariah wrote:

"Many peoples and powerful nations will come to seek ADONAI-Tzva'ot in Jerusalem, and to entreat the favor of ADONAI." Thus says ADONAI-Tzva'ot, "In those days it will come to pass that ten men from every language of the nations will grasp the corner of the garment of a Jew saying, 'Let us go with you, for we have heard that God is with you.'" (Zechariah 8:22–23 TLV)

One day all peoples will grab hold of the Lord by attaching themselves to God's people. When this happens, exile will end and the world will be healed!

On a more personal and practical level, women were not seen as equal to Jewish men. But Jesus and the New Testament make it clear that "there is neither Jew nor Greek, there is neither slave nor free, there is neither male nor female—for you are all one in Messiah *Yeshua*" (Galatians 3:28 TLV). This does not mean there are no longer any differences or distinctions between men and women or Gentiles and Jews; rather, it implies a spiritual equality. There are no second-class citizens in God's kingdom.

CHAPTER 15

CAESAREA PHILIPPI

The Gates of Hades

I tell you that you are Peter, and on this rock I will build
my church, and the gates of Hades will not overcome it.

—MATTHEW 16:18

Caesarea Philippi was an especially pagan city known for its worship of Greek gods and its temples devoted to the ancient god Pan. It was located north of Bethsaida along the Syrian border.

While Jesus and His disciples were in Caesarea Philippi, He asked them an important question:

When Jesus came to the region of Caesarea Philippi, he asked his disciples, "Who do people say the Son of Man is?"

They replied, "Some say John the Baptist; others say Elijah; and still others, Jeremiah or one of the prophets."

"But what about you?" he asked. "Who do you say I am?"

Simon Peter answered, "You are the Messiah, the Son of the living God."

Jesus replied, "Blessed are you, Simon son of Jonah, for this was not revealed to you by flesh and blood, but by my Father in heaven. And I tell you that you are Peter, and on this rock I will build my church, and the gates of Hades will not overcome it." (Matthew 16:13–18)

This Scripture passage has been misunderstood for centuries. Jesus asked His disciples, "Who do you say that I am?" And He is asking the same of us today. Many will respond, "Jesus was a good man." Or "Jesus was a prophet." But Peter answered, "You are the Messiah, the Son of the living God" (v. 16).

The Hebrew word for Messiah means "the Anointed One." Peter meant that Jesus was the long-awaited Savior, spoken of throughout the Old Testament by the prophets, who would come and redeem Israel and save it from its sins.

This was a profound understanding and statement of faith for a simple, uneducated fisherman! The truth of it was stunning, especially in that completely pagan setting. In response, Jesus gave Simon, son of Jonah, a new name: Peter (*petros* in Greek). Here is where many biblical scholars agree that a major misunderstanding occurred centuries ago. The word *petros* describes a shifting, moving rock. The word *petra*, which is used in the next phrase ("and on this rock [*petra*] I will build my church"), is defined as solid rock.

Then Jesus continued, "And the gates of Hades will not overcome it" (v. 18).

Understanding the setting of this biblical scene is essential to understanding the Scriptures. When Jesus posed this question to His disciples, they were likely standing in front of a large pagan temple in Caesarea Philippi called the Gates of Hades. This temple was believed by the Greeks at the time to be the entrance to hell and to the precipitous cavern beneath it, so deep it couldn't be measured.

I don't believe, based on this understanding of the actual words used by Jesus, that Jesus intended to base His church on a man, an imperfect human being, as awesome as Peter was. Because we know very soon from Scripture that this same Peter would deny three times that he even knew Jesus!

Instead, Jesus was saying that He would base His church on the *truth* of what Peter answered: "You are the Messiah, the Son of the living God" (v. 16). This is the *petra*, the solid rock, the cornerstone of the church.

Peter agreed, later saying to the Jewish leaders, "Jesus is 'the stone you builders rejected, which has become the cornerstone'" (Acts 4:11).

In biblical times, a cornerstone was used as the foundation and standard upon which a building was constructed. It was the most important stone in the building process. In fact, the cornerstone was so important that if it were removed, the entire structure could collapse.

Jesus saw deeply into Peter's heart. He saw his love, He saw his faith, and He saw his courage to speak the truth about Jesus, the "Anointed One," the prophesied Messiah. But Jesus also knew that in the near future, on the night before Jesus would be crucified, that same Peter would deny Him three times and later weep bitterly because of his betrayal. Matthew 26:75 tells us, "Then Peter remembered the word Jesus had spoken: 'Before the rooster crows, you will disown me three times.' And he went outside and wept bitterly."

The church, meaning the entire body of Christ—the building of believers—was not built on the frailty of one human being but on the eternal power of the divine Savior of the world, who stood at the very "gates of Hades" in Caesarea Philippi and proclaimed the truth.

Come . . . to Caesarea Philippi!

More from Rabbi Jason

Who Do You Say That I Am?

After leaving the area of Bethesda, Jesus and His disciples went on a thirty-two-mile journey to Caesarea Philippi. To fully understand why Jesus took His disciples on such a long journey to this site, we must understand a bit about the history of this city.

Caesarea Philippi is located on the southern slopes of Mount Hermon in northern Israel. In the time of Joshua, Caesarea was known as Baal Gad (Joshua 11:16–17), named for the fertility god Baal, who was the primary deity worshiped by its inhabitants. The Greek conquest under Alexander the Great led to the hellenization (Greek influence) of Caesarea Philippi and its eventual renaming to Paneas, after the Greek god Pan. Pan was worshiped as the god of the shepherds, flocks, hunters, and mountain wilds, and he was associated with "Pan-ic sex," which was sex for the sake of personal pleasure and lust.

After being conquered by Rome, the city was put under the authority of Herod the Great. In honor of Caesar, Herod built a marble temple that he dedicated to the Roman emperor in 20 BC. Herod's son Philip expanded the city and renamed it Caesarea, to honor Caesar. To distinguish it from Caesarea Maritima, the port city built by Herod, it was referred to as Caesarea Philippi.

Caesarea Philippi is mentioned twice in the New Testament

(Matthew 16:13; Mark 8:27; both accounts of the same event). After arriving in Caesarea Philippi, Jesus asked His disciples, "Who do people say the Son of Man is?" (Matthew 16:13). Then He asked them possibly the most important question found in the Scriptures: "Who do you say I am?" (v. 15).

It seems strange that of all the places that the Lord could have asked this question, He chose Caesarea Philippi. Caesarea Philippi was the "Sin City" of Israel, where the people worshiped Caesar, Baal, and Pan through sexual immorality and wild partying. Yet if you think about it, this was a great location for Jesus to ask His disciples about who they thought He was. These disciples would have been surrounded by temptation as well as the sounds of people proclaiming their allegiance to some of the most popular gods of their day.

It was in this setting that Jesus chose to test not only His disciples' understanding of His identity but also their commitment to Him. Peter responded to His Master's questions by saying, "You are the Messiah, the Son of the living God" (v. 16). Peter's answer was meant to communicate that Jesus was the promised divine, messianic, Davidic king, who alone was to be served.

In response to Peter's great confession, Jesus declared:

"Blessed are you, Simon son of Jonah, for this was not revealed to you by flesh and blood, but by my Father in heaven. And I tell you that you are Peter, and on this rock I will build my church, and the gates of Hades will not overcome it. I will give you the keys of the kingdom of heaven; whatever you bind on earth will be bound in heaven, and whatever you loose on earth will be loosed in heaven." Then he ordered his disciples not to tell anyone that he was the Messiah. (Matthew 16:17–20)

Let's unpack Jesus' response. First, He made it clear that Peter's confession had heavenly origins and was revealed to him by divine inspiration. Peter's statement was not a guess but a God-thought that had been granted to him from above.

Second, as Kathie mentioned above, Jesus made a play on words by using two Greek words, *petros* and *petra*. *Petros* is Peter's Greek name and is best translated as "small stone." *Petra*, on the other hand, means a boulder or foundation stone of a building. Peter, who was a small stone, made a confession of faith that was going to be the huge rock and foundation stone upon which the church would be built. The meaning of the Greek word for "church" used here is *ekklesia* (or *ecclesia*), and its Hebrew equivalent is *edah*, which means "congregation." But what is important here is that the Hebrew word *edah* comes from the Hebrew word *eid*, which means to "bear witness" or "give testimony."

In Jewish thought, there is one key place that the idea of confession and bearing witness are connected. The central Jewish confession of faith is the Shema: "Hear, O Israel: The LORD our God, the LORD is one. Love the LORD your God with all your heart and with all your soul and with all your strength" (Deuteronomy 6:4–5). This declaration is meant to remind us morning and evening that the Lord is the one and only true God. He alone is to be worshiped. By reciting the Shema, Jews declare their loyalty to the King of kings and bear witness to His kingship.

To underscore this bearing-witness component, in Deuteronomy 6:4 there are two letters that are written larger than all others. The first enlarged Hebrew letter is found in the first word, *Shema* (שמע, "hear"); the second larger letter is found in the very last letter of the last word in this verse, which is *echad* (אחד). The enlarged *ayin* of *Shema* and the enlarged *dalet* of *echad* spell *eid*, which is the Hebrew word for "witness"—the same word we looked at above.

What is the point? Peter's confession functioned as a sort of New Testament version of the Shema, which would become a foundational confession of all followers of Messiah. Many of the early Christian martyrs died proclaiming, "Jesus is Lord!"

Jesus then went on to say, concerning the church, that "the gates of Hades will not overcome it" (Matthew 16:18). What exactly was He trying to communicate? A city is only as strong as its gates. In ancient times, cities were protected by walls that usually had one central gate. An invading army attacked the gates of the city since they were the most vulnerable point.

Hades (sometimes called Sheol) is the place where the dead descend after this life. A common belief in antiquity was that there were gates that stood at the entrance to the underworld, which was the realm of the deceased. Once these gates closed, the individual was prevented from experiencing the life of God's kingdom.

The church has been given the mission and the power to break down the gates of death (Hades/Sheol) and open the gates of the kingdom, so that people are delivered from death by declaring, like Peter, that Jesus is the messianic King and Son of God. In Acts 2, during Pentecost, we see that Peter began to use what might be described as "keys of the kingdom" to exercise spiritual authority and unlock the door of salvation by sharing the gospel with Cornelius and his family. Acts 10 tells us that they became the first Gentiles to believe the gospel and be filled with the Holy Spirit.

But there is something more! One day while I was meditating on this verse, I felt the Lord ask me in a still, small voice, *Jason, who do you say I am?* For a moment I was confused. I said, "Lord, You are my Messiah, my Redeemer, and King." But then I realized that this was not actually the question being posed to me. Jesus wanted me to ask Him the opposite: "Lord, who do You say I [Jason] am?" There are so many people who want to define us. And whatever defines us has power over us.

Identity is destiny. If you allow your life to be defined by lies or by people who do not truly know who God created you to be, then you will be robbed of both your true identity and your full destiny. Our identity must come from and be found in the Lord. Like Peter, each one of us must answer Jesus' question, "Who do you say I am?" How we answer this question will shape our eternal destiny for better or worse.

But we also must ask Jesus, "Who am I in Your sight?" In other words, "Who do You say I am based on Your infinite and eternal perspective?" Understanding the answer to these questions on a deep level is a key to experiencing the abundant life Jesus promised us (John 10:10).

CHAPTER 16

THE POOL OF SILOAM

Healing a Blind Man

"Go," he told him, "wash in the Pool of Siloam" (this word means "Sent"). So the man went and washed, and came home seeing.

—JOHN 9:7

The gospel of John tells us that Jesus healed a blind man at the Pool of Siloam (John 9:1–11). The exact location of this pool was debated for centuries until June 2004, when, during construction work to repair a large water pipe south of Jerusalem's Temple Mount at the southern end of a ridge known as the City of David, archaeologists Ronny Reich and Eli Shukron discovered two ancient stone steps. As the work progressed, the excavation revealed that these steps were part of the ancient Pool of Siloam from the Second Temple period, which was during the time of Jesus.

This was no wading pool they had discovered; it measured 225 feet in length. The pool was fed by waters from the Gihon Spring, located in the Kidron Valley. Because these were naturally flowing spring waters, they qualified under Jewish law to be used as a *mikvah*, or ritual bath—something required for all Jews entering the temple to worship.[1]

Adjacent to this extraordinary archaeological find is something equally astounding: Hezekiah's Tunnel, mentioned in 2 Kings 20:20, an amazing underground tunnel that is fascinating to explore. It was used to funnel floodwaters from the temple, but it is widely believed to have also been used as an escape route for the Zealots—the ancient Jewish sect that sought to overthrow the occupying Roman government—when Titus destroyed Jerusalem in AD 70. Evidence suggests that a group of Zealots hid from the Romans deep within adjacent rooms in the tunnel. Carbon-dated bones have been discovered that give credence to this theory.[2]

Rabbi Jason's explanation of the Pool of Siloam once again helps my faith grow ever deeper in a loving God.

Come . . . to the Pool of Siloam!

MORE FROM RABBI JASON

THE MAN BORN BLIND AND DIVINE DNA

Immediately after Jesus left the temple in Jerusalem, He came across a man born blind from birth. Upon seeing this blind man, His disciples asked Him, "Rabbi, who sinned, this man or his parents, that he was born blind?" (John 9:2). Jesus responded that this man's blindness was not the result of any transgression committed by him or his parents. It occurred so that God's power might be brought to light in him.

Jesus then spat in the dirt, made mud with His saliva, placed it on the eyes of the blind man, and told him to go wash in the Pool of Siloam. After washing, the man was miraculously healed and could see for the first time in his life!

We must understand how the Lord performed this miracle to comprehend the full magnitude of this miracle and its deeper message. The most important part of this miracle was the use of saliva to make the mud. This was a man born blind from birth, which means he was born with a genetic defect. He therefore needed to experience healing on both a spiritual and genetic level to be fully cured. If you have ever taken a DNA test or watched an episode of CSI, then you know that one way to get DNA is through saliva. Through His saliva, Jesus was transferring His perfect DNA to this blind man to supernaturally heal him of his genetic defect. In the same way that the Lord created Adam out of the dirt of the ground, Jesus performed a new creation miracle that brought new life to this man.

But there is something more! Jesus' use of spittle was also meant to communicate an important message about His origin and position as God's firstborn Son and legitimate heir to His Father's kingdom. In that culture, the firstborn son was entitled to a double portion of his father's estate. The right of receiving the blessing of the firstborn could be contested if it were proved that the one in question was the firstborn of his mother but not his father, or if he was deemed to be illegitimate because he was born out of wedlock.

There was a belief among some first-century rabbis that the saliva of the firstborn son had healing properties and could be used to prove that the son in question had the right to receive the blessing of the firstborn. There is an example in the Talmud in which a son was proved to be the firstborn because his saliva was used to heal a man's ailing eyes, which was supported by the following statement: "The spittle of the firstborn of a father is healing, but that of the firstborn of a mother is not healing."[3] But this example is minor in comparison to the miracle Jesus performed in John 9. Jesus did not restore the sight to an individual like in the example above, but He actually gave sight to a man who never had it at all. This type of miracle was unheard of and unprecedented; it was a prophetic fulfillment of Isaiah 35:4–5: "Behold, your God! . . . He will save you. Then the eyes of the blind will be opened" (TLV).

There were individuals who questioned the parentage of Jesus and accused Him of being an illegitimate son. Many had doubts about who was His true father. Jesus Himself implied in His teaching that He did not have a human father but a heavenly One. Jesus said He was the One who came from and was sent by the Father. The miraculous healing of the man born blind should have proved Jesus' claim of being God's Son because only the saliva of the Father's firstborn could supernaturally heal in this way. Unfortunately, many of the Judean leaders rejected this sign. The irony is that the one born blind could see, but those who claimed to have a deep knowledge of the Scriptures remained spiritually blind.

Healing this man's eyes demonstrated that Jesus was the promised Messiah, the only begotten Firstborn of our Father in heaven. It also revealed the Lord's overwhelming mercy, kindness, and power! Nothing is impossible with God, even congenital diseases. He truly is the Great Physician! And apart from having our eyes opened by His grace, we remain blind.

CHAPTER 17

THE DECAPOLIS

The Prodigal Son

Not long after that, the younger son got together all he had, set off for a distant country and there squandered his wealth in wild living.

—LUKE 15:13

Many people are familiar with Jesus' parable of the prodigal son, recorded in Luke 15:11–32:

> There was a man who had two sons. The younger one said to his father, "Father, give me my share of the estate." So he divided his property between them.
>
> Not long after that, the younger son got together all he had, set off for a distant country and there squandered his wealth in wild living. After he had spent everything, there was a severe

famine in that whole country, and he began to be in need. So he went and hired himself out to a citizen of that country, who sent him to his fields to feed pigs. He longed to fill his stomach with the pods that the pigs were eating, but no one gave him anything.

When he came to his senses, he said, "How many of my father's hired servants have food to spare, and here I am starving to death! I will set out and go back to my father and say to him: Father, I have sinned against heaven and against you. I am no longer worthy to be called your son; make me like one of your hired servants." So he got up and went to his father.

But while he was still a long way off, his father saw him and was filled with compassion for him; he ran to his son, threw his arms around him and kissed him.

The son said to him, "Father, I have sinned against heaven and against you. I am no longer worthy to be called your son."

But the father said to his servants, "Quick! Bring the best robe and put it on him. Put a ring on his finger and sandals on his feet. Bring the fattened calf and kill it. Let's have a feast and celebrate. For this son of mine was dead and is alive again; he was lost and is found." So they began to celebrate.

Meanwhile, the older son was in the field. When he came near the house, he heard music and dancing. So he called one of the servants and asked him what was going on. "Your brother has come," he replied, "and your father has killed the fattened calf because he has him back safe and sound."

The older brother became angry and refused to go in. So his father went out and pleaded with him. But he answered his father, "Look! All these years I've been slaving for you and never disobeyed your orders. Yet you never gave me even a young goat so I could celebrate with my friends. But when this son of yours who has squandered your property with prostitutes comes home, you kill the fattened calf for him!"

"My son," the father said, "you are always with me, and everything I have is yours. But we had to celebrate and be glad, because this brother of yours was dead and is alive again; he was lost and is found."

Many scholars believe Jesus shared this parable while in Capernaum, just a few miles from the Decapolis, across the Sea of Galilee. The Decapolis (literally "ten cities") is believed to be the place where the seven Canaanite nations who inhabited the land before the Hebrews arrived to conquer it fled to survive Joshua and his army:

- "This is how you will know that the living God is among you and that he will certainly drive out before you the Canaanites, Hittites, Hivites, Perizzites, Girgashites, Amorites and Jebusites" (Joshua 3:10).
- "He overthrew seven nations in Canaan, giving their land to his people as their inheritance" (Acts 13:19).

In Jesus' day, the Decapolis was a Hellenistic (Greek-influenced) area, deeply entrenched in pagan worship and therefore forbidden to any Jew who wished to remain ritually clean, pure, or holy before God. In our vernacular, the setting of this parable would be as if one of our sons left his Christian home for Las Vegas—Sin City, baby! And the prodigal son succumbed to all the depravity that infamous mecca had to offer.

There is an ancient road that follows the coast of the Sea of Galilee from Capernaum to the Decapolis. In this parable, it is note-worthy that the father saw his son returning home from "a long way off" (Luke 15:20) and picked up his robe and ran for joy toward his precious "sin-soaked" son. In Jesus' day, the father's action would have shocked his audience. No decent Jewish man would be so immodest as to lift his robe, nor would he embarrass himself by running toward a son who had brought him and the family so much shame. By all rights, the prodigal son should have been dead to him. But the beauty of it is the exact opposite! His son was alive! He was coming home, and he was sorry! The father simply could not contain his glorious joy.

Of course, the father in this parable is a metaphor for God, our heavenly Father, and how He acts whenever one of us, His children, repents and returns to the Father's House (see "Bet Av" on page 122). In Luke 15:7, Jesus said, "I tell you that in the same way there will be more rejoicing in heaven over one sinner who repents than over ninety-nine righteous persons who do not need to repent."

The father in the story embraced his son with total abandon, oblivious to the stench of the sweat and the pigs and the debauchery. He called for the fattened calf to be butchered for a homecoming feast; he threw his best robe over his son's filth, and he put his signet ring on the son's grimy finger, signifying the son's place of importance in the family. The father put shoes on his son's feet. He treated him as royalty instead of what he actually was: an ingrate, a degenerate, and a profound disappointment to everyone, mostly his father.

This story is one of the most moving examples of a father's mercy in all of literature. As you are standing in Capernaum, it is easy to imagine the extraordinary scene that Jesus described just up the ancient road.

But lost in many sermons on this parable is the story of the older son—the "good" son—who came home from working hard in his father's field to the sound of music and merriment and rejoicing.

When told the news of his brother's unexpected return, the older son became belligerent, hurt, and combative. He refused to go into the party to welcome his brother home. Some would say he had good reason. After all, the older son didn't cause his father pain, embarrassment, disappointment, or sorrow.

I believe this son represents those of us who are "Pharisees" in our hearts. We keep all the rules, we do everything required of us, and we are faithful and loyal believers. But we lack what our Father cares about most: love, compassion, mercy, grace, and forgiveness. These are the things the prodigal son's father expressed to his beloved son—who was once lost but now is found.

This is a perfect picture of redemption. We can only imagine the reaction of the Pharisees in Jesus' audience that day. Did they recognize themselves in the person of the unloving but faithful son?

Do we?

Come . . . to the Decapolis!

CHAPTER 18

THE MOUNT OF OLIVES

The Triumphal Entry

*When he came near the place where the road goes down the
Mount of Olives, the whole crowd of disciples began joyfully
to praise God in loud voices for all the miracles they had seen:
"Blessed is the king who comes in the name of the Lord!"*

—LUKE 19:37–38

The Mount of Olives, or Mount Olivet, is part of a mountain
ridge east of and adjacent to the Old City of Jerusalem. Olive
groves once covered its slopes, and a small grove—the Garden of
Gethsemane—remains there to this day. What surprises some first-
time visitors is that this place has been used as a Jewish cemetery for
more than three thousand years. Many Jews believe the Messiah will
someday arrive in Jerusalem through the Mount of Olives—and

when He does, the dead will rise from their graves and walk to the Temple Mount. Therefore, many Jewish believers wish to be buried at this site, only a few meters away from the Old City, with their feet facing the Temple Mount.[1] Headstones are arranged row after row, representing approximately 150,000 graves, creating an almost surreal tableau as you face the city of Jerusalem while standing on the Mount of Olives.

The Mount of Olives is one of my favorite places in all of Israel, for it features prominently in the Scriptures in the life of Jesus. Yet according to the Bible, the Mount of Olives will also play an important role in the second coming of Jesus during the end times.

There are a few areas on the Mount of Olives that are nothing short of thrilling for me.

One of them is the ancient road that descends from the top of the mountain to the bottom at the foot of the Kidron Valley. This is the road on which Jesus rode on the foal of a donkey on Palm Sunday, the last week of His life. To the left, you can see many ancient graves, which brings to mind the time when Jesus was criticized because the people were waving palm leaves and crying, "Blessed is the king who comes in the name of the Lord!" (Luke 19:38). Some of the Pharisees in the crowd became angry and told Jesus, "Teacher, rebuke your disciples!" (v. 39). Jesus answered, "I tell you, if they [the people] keep quiet, the stones will cry out" (v. 40).

It's deeply moving to walk this ancient road, knowing that these very graves were the stones Jesus was referring to. Along the short way down, Scripture tells us in Matthew 23:37 that Jesus saw the magnificent city before Him and exclaimed, "Jerusalem, Jerusalem, you who kill the prophets and stone those sent to you, how often I have longed to gather your children together, as a hen gathers her chicks under her wings, and you were not willing."

Jesus knew exactly what was to befall Him in the week ahead. Yet His every spoken word was about His concern for others, not for Himself. That would come later, on His last night on earth during the agony of the Garden of Gethsemane.

One of the most profound teachings I've ever received happened during our tour of Israel at a specific place on the Mount of Olives.

It was unusual for Ray to care much where we sat, as long as we were comfortable and within earshot. But on this day, he had all eighteen of us sit on a stone wall with our backs to a very bushy area, looking out facing south. It couldn't have been more than thirty feet from one end of us to the other. Because Ray had never arranged us this way, we were already intrigued.

"I want you to look directly behind you," Ray began. "See all that overgrown bush there against that wall?"

We could all see it perfectly. The wall that the foliage was growing on was barely visible it was so pervasive.

Ray directed our attention back to him as he pulled out his wallet and took out a small laminated card, the size of a driver's license.

"Look here." He pointed at the tiny black speck in the middle of the card. "See this?"

We could all barely make it out.

"That," he explained, "is a mustard seed, among the smallest seeds in all of the botanical world. It's smaller than a speck of pepper."

He let that settle in, and it truly was extraordinary to wrap our minds around it.

"Now," he said, "look back at all that growth behind you again."

Naturally, we obeyed, wondering where all this was going.

"That is the most feared plant in all of Israel, the mustard plant. It's feared because once it takes root it can't be destroyed. You can try to burn it out, stomp it out, tear it out, but eventually it takes over everything in its way."

Ray paused, lifted up his Bible, and said: "The mustard seed is the kingdom of God! Once it gets planted, nothing can stop it! I wonder if the disciples made the connection to Jesus' other teaching—that if we have faith even as small as this, we can say to that mountain. . . ." He pointed to something we hadn't noticed before: Herodium in the distance!

". . . Be gone! And it will be thrown into that sea!"

Now we looked where he was pointing at a stunning image: the Dead Sea!

Ray reminded us that the rabbis always taught what the simple people could see and hear and smell and taste and touch. The weight of what he was teaching was overwhelming: this is the only spot on the Mount of Olives where these three things—the mustard plant, Herodium, and the Dead Sea—are visible.

Thus, Jesus had to have been standing *right there* when He shared this parable!

We all just sat there, stunned.

I could easily picture Jesus standing exactly where Ray was standing. I moved my eyes behind me there, then to my right, then before me again—and I began to weep.

Ray continued: "The kingdom of God is us! It is all of us as believers. If we just believe, we can say to that mountain—the world's way, Herod's way, Satan's way—be gone, into that sea, the Dead Sea, which is already dead!"

Come . . . to the Mount of Olives!

MORE FROM RABBI JASON

THE TRIUMPHAL ENTRY AT THE MOUNT OF OLIVES

Jesus rode down the Mount of Olives into Jerusalem on a donkey during what has become known as the Triumphal Entry. But did you ever wonder why He chose to ride on a donkey? Every one of Jesus' actions was intentional. He came to fulfill everything that was prophesied by Moses and the prophets concerning the Messiah so that the world might know that He was the promised Redeemer.

Speaking of the coming Messiah, the Old Testament prophet Zechariah wrote:

Rejoice greatly, daughter of *Zion*!
Shout, daughter of Jerusalem!
Behold, your king is coming to you,
a righteous one bringing salvation.
He is lowly, riding on a donkey—
on a colt, the foal of a donkey. (Zechariah 9:9 TLV)

So Jesus the Messiah came riding on a donkey in fulfillment of this prophecy. But there is much more meaning as to why a donkey was chosen. Horses are a symbol of military might, wealth, and strength. Donkeys, on the other hand, are symbolic of humility and peace. At His first coming, Messiah came as the humble lamb of God riding on a donkey. But at His second coming, He will descend from the heavens riding a white warhorse ready to vanquish all evil from the world (Revelation 19:11–16).

Still deeper, the donkey plays a key role in the history of the redemption of God's people. We see this in the life of Abraham, the father of the Christian faith. Abraham in Hebraic thought went through ten tests. The final test was the offering of Isaac upon the altar as a sacrifice to the Lord, which demonstrated his great faith (Hebrews 11). But it was also meant to paint a portrait of God the Father's willingness to offer His only Son on our behalf. In Genesis 22, Abraham put his supplies on a donkey when he went on the three-day journey to offer Isaac, who was a type (or symbolic figure) of Messiah, as a burnt offering on Mount Moriah (Genesis 22:3).

Moses also made use of a donkey when he was sent by God to redeem the children of Israel from Egypt. In Exodus 4:20, Moses put his wife and children on a donkey.

Abraham's and Moses' use of a donkey was ultimately meant to point to the Messiah who would also use a donkey when He came to usher in the start of the messianic kingdom that would come through His sufferings.

Jesus' riding on a donkey not only underscored His humility, but also pointed to the fact that He was the greater Abraham. As Jesus said, "Abraham rejoiced to see My day; he saw it and was thrilled" (John 8:56 TLV). Jesus was also the greater prophet like Moses, who came to bring about an even greater redemption (Acts 3:22). Thus the work of redemption that began with Abraham and was taken to the next level by Moses was advanced further by Jesus, who at His Second Coming will bring complete transformation to all of creation.

When you truly welcome Jesus into your life as King and Savior, like the crowd seemed to do during His Triumphal Entry—crying out, "Blessed is the king who comes in the name of the Lord!" (Luke 19:38)— you begin to experience not only personal salvation, but also real new-creation transformation.

Gezer, next to the Via Maris—the ancient trade route known as the "Road of the Sea."

Gezer is really our first stop right off the plane in Tel Aviv. It's a lot steeper of a climb than it appears.

En Gedi. The glorious oasis in the desert next to the Dead Sea. David hid near here from King Saul and wrote many of his psalms in the caves deep within the Rock.

En Gedi. The sheer beauty of it is astounding and totally worth the steep, hot climb.

En Gedi. David's waterfall.

The Judean Desert in the afternoon.

Caesarea Maritima.
Herod's brilliant
man-made harbor,
ready to receive
Caesar's ships.

Caesarea Maritima. The amphitheater and
sports complex known as the Hippodrome.

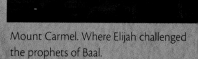

Mount Carmel. Where Elijah challenged
the prophets of Baal.

The Sea of Galilee.
Beyond beautiful!

Mount Carmel. This is what the mustard plant looks like at its peak in the spring.

Mount Arbel. One of the ancient paths.

Mount Arbel. This is at the top, with the Sea of Galilee in the distance.

Mount of Olives. See the Kidron Valley at the base of the mountain.

Mount of Olives. With my three favorite people in the world: Cody Gifford, Cassidy Gifford, and Christine Gardner.

Mount of Olives. Some of the ancient graves in the Kidron Valley.

Mount of Olives. The ancient road Jesus rod down on Palm Sunday.

…e Garden of Gethsemane. Virtually …nchanged since Jesus prayed here to be …livered from the suffering ahead—"yet not …y will, but yours be done."

Herodium. Herod's palace near Bethlehem. Breathtaking.

…e Jericho Road. Jesus and His disciples …veled it when they "went up to Jerusalem."

Arad in the Negev Desert. Where God made His covenant with Abraham.

…e Church of the Holy Sepulchre. Where …st scholars believe Jesus was crucified and …urrected.

The Via Dolorosa. Marking the stations of the cross.

Jerusalem. An ancient road in the Arab section of the city.

The Dead Sea. An evening view.

The Temple Mount. The most sacred site in Israel for Jews and Muslims.

Jerusalem. Near the Western Wall.

Masada. The famous cable to the top.

Masada (seen in the top-right corner). It was Herod's favorite palace.

Masada. For those who choose the hard way to the summit. Most take the cable car.

Masada. One of several water cisterns. Another example of Herod's architectural genius.

Qumran. Next to the Dead Sea, where the ancient Essenes wrote and hid the famous Dead Sea Scrolls.

Qumran. The actual caves—site of one of the greatest archaeological discoveries of our time.

Modern-day Bethlehem. Seen from Herod's palace at Herodium.

Bet Shean, in the Decapolis. A place forbidden to the ancient Jews, yet Jesus came here to save a demon-possessed man because He loved him.

Chorazin. One of the sites where an ancient synagogue has been discovered.

The Jordan River. In all its glory.

My daughter Cassidy's baptism in the Jordan River. Our precious brothers Remi Adeleke and Rod Van Solkema holding her against the strong current.

My son Cody's baptism in the Jordan River. He is forever bonded with these two amazing men of God.

During His Triumphal Entry into Jerusalem from the Mount of Olives, Jesus wept over the city. He saw that it would be destroyed because the people did not recognize or receive Him as the promised Messiah, the one spoken of by Moses and the prophets (Luke 19:39–44). The Mount of Olives is the location of the Olivet Discourse, in which Jesus described the prophetic future of Jerusalem and some of the key signs of the end times (Matthew 24–25; Mark 13; Luke 21:5–36).

Perhaps most importantly, it was from the Mount of Olives that Jesus ascended into heaven forty days after His resurrection (Acts 1:9–12). Of all the locations Jesus could have chosen to ascend from, why did He choose this place and not a more prominent one, such as the Temple Mount?

The prophetic significance of the Mount of Olives is likely the primary reason the Lord chose this site as the place of His ascension. The prophet Ezekiel saw God's glory depart from the Temple of Solomon and Jerusalem by way of the Mount of Olives (Ezekiel 11:22–23). Ezekiel also prophetically saw the Lord's glorious presence returning from the east, coming over the Mount of Olives, and entering into the future messianic temple of God (Ezekiel 43:1–5).

Finally, Zechariah prophesied that at the coming of Messiah, "His feet will stand on the Mount of Olives which lies to the east of Jerusalem, and the Mount of Olives will be split in two from east to west" (Zechariah 14:4 TLV). Messiah's ascent to heaven was meant as a precursor and sneak preview of His ultimate return, as described in Zechariah. This was confirmed by the angels in Acts 1:11, who said to the disciples, "Men of Galilee, . . . why do you stand here looking into the sky? This same Jesus, who has been taken from you into heaven, will come back in the same way you have seen him go into heaven."

We must actively look for, long for, and pray for the Messiah's coming, like the apostles who watched Him ascend into heaven. Think how your life would be changed if you passionately longed for and lived every day as if this would be the moment Jesus would return!

CHAPTER 19

THE UPPER ROOM

The Passover Seder

*"Say to the master of the house, 'The Teacher says, "Where
is the guest room in which I may eat the Passover with My
disciples?"' Then he will show you a large upper room,
furnished and prepared; there make ready for us."*

—MARK 14:14—15 NKJV

I have visited the Armenian section of Jerusalem, where the traditional sites of the Tomb of David and the Upper Room are believed to be, though there is little there now to confirm it. However, we know clearly from Scripture what took place in the Upper Room.

I'm going to let Rabbi Jason lead us through this section about the room that would change history forever.

Come . . . to the Upper Room!

MORE FROM RABBI JASON

THE LAST SUPPER, PASSOVER, AND THE UPPER ROOM

The Upper Room is the site of many important events in the lives of Jesus and the apostles. As Passover approached, the disciples asked Jesus, "Where do You want us to go and prepare for You to eat the Passover?" (Mark 14:12 TLV). Jesus responded by saying that they would see a man carrying a jar of water and that this man "will show you a large upper room, furnished and ready" (v. 15 TLV). This final meal that Jesus ate with His disciples, commonly referred to as the Last Supper, was really a Passover Seder (ceremonial meal) that Jesus and His disciples celebrated. Not only did Jesus eat the Passover with His disciples, but He also taught them how the key elements of the Passover Seder pointed to and found their ultimate fulfillment in Him.

The Passover Seder is a special meal eaten on Passover, centered around drinking four cups of wine (or grape juice). Each of the four cups has deep spiritual significance and symbolizes the four distinct promises God made to the Jewish people in Exodus 6:6–7.

The first cup is known as the cup of sanctification. Jesus began His Seder by reciting the blessing over this first cup. We read about this in Luke 22:17–18: "And when He had taken a cup and offered the *bracha* [blessing], He said, 'Take this and share it among yourselves'" (TLV). During a Passover Seder, we respond to the cup of sanctification by crying out, "God, make us holy. Set us apart for Your plans and holy purposes for our lives."

The second cup is commonly referred to as the cup of plagues. During this part of the Passover meal, we remember that God redeemed us with great signs and great wonders. We remember that

God, through Moses, turned water into blood, and that Messiah's first miracle turned water into wine because He is greater than Moses.

The third cup is known as the cup of redemption. When we drink this cup, we are reminded of the blood of the Passover lamb that was put upon the doorposts of the house. At the Passover Seder, when Jesus blessed the cup and gave it to His disciples, He did that with this third cup, the cup of redemption. He said to His disciples, "Drink from it, all of you; for this is My blood of the covenant, which is poured out for many for the removal of sins" (Matthew 26:27–28 TLV).

Blood played a central role in Israel's deliverance from bondage in Egypt. God told the children of Israel that in order to be spared from the final and worst plague, the death of the firstborn, they would have to slaughter a lamb and place its blood on the doorposts of their home. Any family that failed to do so would lose their firstborn in this plague. Just as the blood on the doorposts of the house in Egypt saved Israel from the plague of the death of the firstborn, those who belong to Jesus have been bought by the blood of the Lamb of God. We do not have to experience the wrath of God and His judgment because Jesus died for us as the ultimate Passover lamb! Whenever we partake of the Lord's Supper, we are symbolically drinking and spiritually partaking of the third cup, the cup of redemption.

The fourth cup is the cup of acceptance or thanksgiving. This cup looks to the future, to the coming of the kingdom. It was over the fourth cup that Jesus said, "I will never drink of this fruit of the vine from now on, until that day when I drink it anew with you in My Father's kingdom" (v. 29 TLV). When we drink the fourth cup in the Passover Seder, we acknowledge and give thanks for our acceptance as children of the King, knowing our position, power, and authority in Messiah.

A second key element of the Passover is the *matzah*, the unleavened bread (plural, *matzot*). *Matzah* is to be eaten for seven days during Passover and serves as a reminder that God brought Israel "out from the land of Egypt in haste" (Deuteronomy 16:3 TLV). *Matzah* bread has almost a corrugated look, with holes like dotted lines running vertically alongside rows of browned pockets of dough. *Matzah* is symbolic of both redemption and affliction. The affliction that the bread represents is the centuries of slavery in Egypt endured by the children of Israel. The brown stripes running the length of the bread recall the lashings of Israel's taskmasters in Egypt. It is also known as the bread of freedom and healing, when God redeemed His people from Egypt with an "outstretched arm" (Exodus 6:6 TLV).

We can also see Jesus represented in the *matzah*. See Isaiah 53:4–5:

> Surely he took up our pain
> and bore our suffering,
> yet we considered him punished by God,
> stricken by him, and afflicted.
> But he was pierced for our transgressions, . . .
> the punishment that brought us peace was on him,
> and by his wounds [stripes, NKJV] we are healed.

Jesus' "bread of affliction" was the weight of our sins. The *matzah's* holes stand for His piercings, and the brown stripes represent His stripes by which we are healed and set free from bondage to sin and our own "Egypts." These are personal prisons that confine and limit us from being who God wants us to be and doing what He has destined for us.

The *matzah* is broken during the fourth step in the Seder called *yachatz*, which means "to break." During the Last Supper, *matzah* was the bread Jesus lifted, broke, and "gave it to his disciples, saying, 'Take and eat; this is my body'" (Matthew 26:26). In fact, communion can be seen as a mini-Passover each time we partake. Did you realize there was such deep meaning in so thin a cracker?

A third key traditional element of the Passover Seder that was also part of the Last Supper was the bitter herbs (*maror*, in Hebrew). God commanded Israel to commemorate the Passover with *matzah* and bitter herbs (Exodus 12:8; Numbers 9:11). The bitter herbs are meant to remind us of how the Egyptians embittered the lives of our ancestors with hard labor (Exodus 1:14). The most commonly used bitters include romaine lettuce, horseradish, and endives.

Whether you eat a fresh slice of horseradish or a leaf of romaine lettuce, you should be thinking of the bitterness of slavery during *maror*. Traditionally, we dip the *maror* in the *charoset* (the apple-nut-wine-cinnamon mixture that represents the mortar used for the bricks) to taste a small amount of sweetness along with the bitter flavor. One reason for this is that even during the most bitter years of slavery, the promise of redemption that God made to Abraham added sweetness to Israel's suffering.

On the night Jesus was betrayed, John 13:25–27 shows how He revealed His betrayer:

Then he who leaned on *Yeshua's* chest says to Him, "Master, who is it?"

Yeshua answers, "It's the one I will give this bit of *matzah* to, after I dip it." After dipping the *matzah*, He takes it and gives it to Judah from Kriot, the son of Simon. And with that bit, satan entered into him. Then *Yeshua* tells him, "What you're about to do, do quickly!" (TLV)

So in addition to the bitterness of slavery, this step during the Passover Seder represents the bitterness of separation from Jesus as exemplified by Judas.

A fourth element, and the most central element of the Seder in the first century, was the Passover lamb. The command to eat the Passover lamb is first found in Exodus 12:8, which states: "They are to eat the meat that night, roasted over a fire. With *matzot* and bitter herbs they are to eat it" (TLV). The offering of the Passover lamb was meant to be a reminder of blood placed on the doorposts of the Israelites' homes in Egypt.

But not just any lamb would be acceptable to be eaten in fulfillment of the commandment of Passover. The Passover lamb had to be slaughtered as a sacrifice to the Lord (*korban*, in Hebrew), in the designated location that had been chosen for offerings. Deuteronomy 16:5–6 states: "You may not sacrifice the Passover offering within any of your gates that ADONAI your God is giving you. Rather, at the place ADONAI your God chooses to make His Name dwell, there you will sacrifice the Passover offering in the evening at sunset—the time of your coming out from Egypt" (TLV).

Since the destruction of the second Jerusalem temple by the Romans in AD 70, there has been no Passover sacrifice offered in the fulfillment of this prophecy. For this reason, Jews of European descent don't eat lamb today and will not do so until the temple in Jerusalem is restored.

Jesus taught that He was the true Passover lamb and the promised Messiah who came to bring about a greater Exodus. Moses came to redeem Israel from slavery in Egypt, but Messiah Jesus came to bring deliverance from sin and death. From the perspective of the New Testament, true freedom is found in God's Son, Jesus, of whom it is written, "If the Son sets you free, you will be free indeed!" (John 8:36 TLV).

God the Father sent His Son, Jesus, so that everyone who receives and believes in Him might find freedom and everlasting life in the world to come! Just like Israel had to apply the blood of the Passover lamb to the doorposts of their homes so that death would pass over their first-born sons, so every one of us must apply the blood of Jesus, the greater Passover Lamb of God, so that death and judgment will pass over us!

CHAPTER 20

BET AV

The Father's House

My Father's house has many rooms; if that were not so, would I have told you that I am going there to prepare a place for you?

—JOHN 14:2

I wish everyone could go on a Rock and Road Experience trip to Israel with Rod Van Solkema and his beautiful wife, Libby. They are an amazing team. Rod is a pastor in Grand Rapids, Michigan, but he thinks of himself more as a coach. It's obvious on a trip with him that he is both. He is also a compassionate, passionate lover of Jesus and the Word of God.

Libby is not only a great support system for Rod, but she is also an excellent, gifted teacher as well. I always looked forward to the times when Rod would ask Libby to share one of her parables with the group. Together, they are a beautiful example of a godly marriage. And they are a force to be reckoned with!

Rod studied under Ray Vander Laan, and Ray told me that he considers Rod to be one of his greatest students ever. One of my favorite teachings I heard from Rod was about how Abraham instigated the ancient tradition of Bet Av—in Hebrew, "the house of the father." Another translation would be "father's household."

Rod Van Solkema teaches that all of Scripture is about Bet Av— "The Father's House."

God longs for every human being to come into His house and to know His love and care. It is only when we find our place in His family that we find joy and peace and salvation.

In biblical times, a Jewish home was headed by the father. The father had supreme rights over his children and could marry off his daughters, divorce his wife, arrange marriages for his sons, and even sell his children, which is a very difficult thing to comprehend in our modern times.

But in God's plan, the father is there to protect and provide for his family in every way.

Basically, the concept of Bet Av includes your family and your extended family—your father, mother, brothers, sisters, cousins, aunts, and uncles. All your relatives. It's a life arrangement in which everything and everyone are under the care and the protection of the patriarch. It is his job as the father to meet every need of his household.

Take a moment and put yourself in that world. Imagine that the Bet Av is everything to you. The father's house is your protection, your security, your meaning, your happiness, your identity—your very life.

To lose your Bet Av is to lose everything. God, in His wisdom, created the Bet Av as a paradigm of His kingdom, for He is our heavenly Father and our sovereign Protector.

Central to the Jewish Bet Av is the concept of redemption—though not in the sense of redemption from sin. This concept of redemption refers to redeeming what is lost, bringing it back into the Bet Av. For example, say a family member lost a piece of property, went bankrupt, or became marginalized in some way. If that happened, it was the father's responsibility to use all his resources to bring that person back into the Bet Av and to restore that man or woman to safety and security. The father would do whatever it takes to "redeem" his family member.

It's the same in modern times. God is our Redeemer. He says to us, "Do not fear, for I have redeemed you; I have summoned you by name; you are mine" (Isaiah 43:1). This is what God is saying to each of us today, at this very moment!

To those of us who are alienated from home, marginalized, cast out, or lost, God is crying out: *I am your Father! I will do anything to buy you back, restore you to my family.* Or as Jeremiah 29:11 says, "to give you hope and a future."

Our heavenly Father made this possible by sending His only Son, Jesus—His most precious resource—to seek us out, to find us, and to show us the face of the Father who loves us with an all-consuming love. In Hebrews 1:3 we read, "The Son is the radiance of God's glory and the exact representation of his being, sustaining all things by his powerful word."

Jesus died so that we could be redeemed from sin and rejoin the Father's family. The Holy Trinity is a family—Father, Son, and Holy Spirit—and we have been born into an eternal Bet Av by the Father's mercy and grace.

In John 14:2, Jesus was teaching about the Bet Av. He told His disciples, "In My Father's house are many mansions" (NKJV). However, this is an example of a poor translation of Scripture. The word *mansions* in some translations of John 14:2 implies a life of lavish privilege, living in heaven on streets of gold. But it is the exact opposite. It is a picture of the church becoming the bride of Christ.

The Bible talks about how Jesus is the lover of our soul in Song of Solomon 1–2, using the concept of marriage as a picture and an expression of the unity and intimacy that completes a human being. Jeremiah 3:14 describes us as being married to the Lord. In heaven, our concept of earthly marriage will be replaced by a heavenly, perfect marriage to the One who gave Himself in love for us. What a concept!

A better Greek translation of John 14:2 is "rooms," not mansions: "My Father's house has many rooms." In this passage, Jesus is referring to Bet Av as it related to Jewish wedding customs. In ancient times, the father's house was designed to be able to add a room for a newly married son. After an engagement, the prospective groom would return to his father's house and begin to build a new room for himself and his bride. That's why Jesus told His disciples, "I go to prepare a place for you" (John 14:2 NKJV).

After the marriage, the groom and his bride would be given this new room as their own—a place where they could privately explore their new life together in an intimate setting. In this fashion, the Bet Av, or father's house, would continue to grow as the family did.

Come . . . to the Father's house!

CHAPTER 21

GARDEN OF GETHSEMANE

"Not My Will, but Yours"

*He withdrew about a stone's throw beyond them, knelt
down and prayed, "Father, if you are willing, take this
cup from me; yet not my will, but yours be done."*

—LUKE 22:41–42

Gethsemane means "oil press." The Garden of Gethsemane is
mentioned in Matthew 26:36: "Then Jesus went with his
disciples to a place called Gethsemane, and he said to them, 'Sit here
while I go over there and pray.'"

Mark 14:32 says it like this: "They went to a place called
Gethsemane, and Jesus said to his disciples, 'Sit here while I pray.'"

In Aramaic, Gethsemane is a place or enclosed piece of ground
to which Jesus and His disciples retired. In John 18:1, this place

is described as a garden (*kepos,* in Greek): "When he had finished praying, Jesus left with his disciples and crossed the Kidron Valley. On the other side there was a garden, and he and his disciples went into it."

Scholars dispute the exact location of the Garden of Gethsemane, but that didn't spoil our tour group's experience. We know it could be anywhere in a general area, so it didn't really matter to me where it was exactly. It was there, somewhere close, and no academic argument can mar the experience for me or millions of others who seek Him.

On the Mount of Olives, right next to the Church of Mary Magdalene, there is an ancient grotto where an equally ancient gethsemane, or oil press, still exists. It is here that many scholars believe Jesus and His disciples spent the last week before Jesus' crucifixion.

Once deep inside this beautiful grotto, it is not difficult to accept that this could, indeed, be the actual place where Jesus and His disciples slept before Jesus was betrayed by Judas, arrested, and led to His suffering at the hands of the Sanhedrin and Pontius Pilate.

Come . . . to the Garden of Gethsemane!

More from Rabbi Jason

Gethsemane, Eden, and the Anointed One

After celebrating Passover, Jesus and His disciples walked to the Mount of Olives, to the Garden of Gethsemane (Matthew 26:36). The fact that Jesus spent the final hours before His arrest in a garden is significant. First, the fall of man occurred in a garden—so Jesus, who is the second Adam, also entered into a garden as He prepared to give His life to atone for the sin of the first man and woman.

Second, one of the primary titles ascribed to Jesus is "Christ." Growing up, I thought this was His last name. Instead, Christ is the Greek equivalent of the Hebrew word *Mashiach* (Messiah), which means "the Anointed One." Why is this so significant? In ancient Israel, kings were anointed with olive oil as a sign of being chosen and empowered by God to rule. Thus, the term *Messiah* in Judaism came to refer to the promised messianic King and Redeemer who would be anointed with olive oil and, more importantly, by the Spirit of the Lord to establish the kingdom of God.

According to Isaiah, it is out of an olive stump that "a shoot will come forth out of the stem of Jesse, and a branch will bear fruit out of His roots," and "the *Ruach* of ADONAI [Spirit of the Lord] will rest upon Him" as the anointed Messiah from the line of David (Isaiah 11:1–2 TLV). It's amazing to think that Jesus spent one of the most important moments of His life in an olive garden, which is the very type of tree that was most symbolic of His role as Messiah (Jeremiah 33:15; Zechariah 3:8; 6:12).

As Kathie explained, Gethsemane comes from the Aramaic word meaning "olive press." Olives went through three pressings to remove every ounce of oil. The three pressings of the olives are connected to the three times Jesus asked His heavenly Father to "let this cup pass from Me" (Matthew 26:39, 42, 44 TLV). Like an olive in a press, Jesus was being crushed by the weight of humanity's sin, so that by His pressing of the oil, the light of salvation might be released into our lives. The crushing that Jesus experienced for you and me was so severe that He sweated blood (Luke 22:44).

But there is something more! Jesus asked His three closest disciples—Peter, James, and John—to watch and pray with Him (Matthew 26:38). At the start of Messiah's ministry, He was led into the desert, where while fasting and praying He was tested three times by Satan. At the end of His ministry, Jesus seemed to be undergoing a final and similar test. While it was important for Him to pass the test, He wanted His disciples, especially Peter, to gain the spiritual strength needed to pass the test as well.

Three times the disciples fell asleep, even though the Lord asked them to tarry with Him in prayer. Jesus knew Satan wanted to sift Peter and the disciples like wheat but, would not be able to due to His intercession for them (Luke 22:32). Jesus wanted the disciples to pray with Him so that they might be able to resist temptation. This is only speculation, but perhaps Jesus hoped that if Peter had tarried with Him in prayer for those last few hours and had not fallen asleep three times, he would have had the strength to not deny Him three times.

All of us must be vigilant to watch and pray so that we don't succumb to the temptation to deny the Lord when we go through the olive presses of life and feel like we are being crushed by our situation and circumstances. We must remember that it is the crushing that brings out the true inner value and worth of the olive, which is the oil.

CHAPTER 22

GOLGOTHA

The Triumph of the Cross

*Carrying his own cross, he went out to the place of the Skull (which
in Aramaic is called Golgotha). There they crucified him, and
with him two others—one on each side and Jesus in the middle.*

—JOHN 19:17–18

W hen we were screening Mel Gibson's movie *The Passion of the
Christ* at our home, I began to sob uncontrollably during the
scene where Jesus falls and, in spite of His agony, says to His mother:
"Behold, Mother. I make all things new." My daughter, Cassidy,
who was eleven years old at the time, said: "Don't cry, Mommy. It
has a happy ending, remember?"

Don't you just love the innocence and truth of children? But
what she didn't understand was that I wasn't crying tears of pain,

but tears of joy. She was right, of course. It *does* have a happy ending because of Jesus' sacrifice. He made eternal life possible for every human being.

I have read the biblical account of Jesus' arrest, "trial," scourging, and crucifixion hundreds of times. I take comfort in knowing that account is based on eyewitness testimonies by the Gospel writers. Many scholars believe the gospel of Mark to be one of the earliest writings in the New Testament, most probably written to Christian believers in Rome before the destruction of Jerusalem in AD 70. Mark begins his gospel by declaring that Jesus was the Messiah long prophesied in the Old Testament; thus, He is the Son of the living God, the Anointed One, the long-awaited deliverer of Israel.

Interestingly, I learned that the biblical narrative of Jesus' last day on earth parallels almost exactly what was known as the Roman Triumph. What originally was seen as a tragic defeat for Jesus and His kingdom was eventually found to be the exact opposite: the greatest triumph in history.

The Bible tells us that Jesus was born during the reign of the Roman emperor Caesar Augustus, who was the son of the assassinated Julius Caesar. Caesar Augustus vowed to build a temple to honor his murdered father and to hold a dedication ceremony to proclaim his father as divine. During that ceremony, a comet streaked through the sky—a sign that Caesar Augustus declared as confirmation that he himself must be "the Son of God," if his father, Julius Caesar, was God. From that period on, the Roman people believed Caesar Augustus to be the divine "Son of God."

What began as a way to honor conquering generals soon became limited to the emperors, proclaiming their sovereignty and divinity. The ceremony began with the Roman soldiers who assembled at the Praetorium, where the guards were stationed. Then a purple robe (the color of royalty) would be placed on the emperor and a wreath would be placed on his head. "Hail Caesar!" they would shout, and the people would chant, "Triomphe!" as the emperor and the guards wound their way along the Via Sacra in Rome to arrive at the Capitoline, or "head hill." There, a bull would be sacrificed by someone who had been carrying an instrument of death.

The emperor would then be offered a bowl of wine, which he would refuse or sometimes pour out on the head of the sacrificial bull.

Finally, the emperor would ascend the steps of the Capitoline, accompanied by someone on his left and someone on his right.

The entire population would declare him as their "savior"— their divine Caesar, proclaiming, "Hail Caesar, Lord and God!" Then they would all look for signs in the heavens to confirm their leader's coronation.

Ray brilliantly described how the description of Jesus' last days in Mark's gospel, including Jesus' suffering, perfectly paralleled the Roman procession known as a triumph.

After Jesus had been sentenced to death by Pontius Pilate, He was taken to the Praetorium in Jerusalem by the Roman guards. There, they stripped Him, threw a purple robe over Him, and placed a crown of thorns on His head. Then they mockingly worshiped Him, shouting, "Hail, the King of the Jews" and bowed down to Him, striking Him and spitting on Him.

After they had tired of this sport, they led Him away along the Via Dolorosa to be crucified. Jesus carried His own cross (instrument of death) until He collapsed beneath it. A passerby, Simon of Cyrene, was forced to carry Jesus' cross for Him to Golgotha ("the Place of the Skull").

There, the soldiers laid Jesus on the cross and crucified Him along with two revolutionaries, one on His left and one on His right. They offered Him sour wine, which He refused.

Pontius Pilate had insisted that a sign (a *titulus*—a placard that identified His so-called crime) reading "THE KING OF JEWS" be nailed to Jesus' cross. As He suffered, the crowd around Him taunted Him, "Hail, the King of the Jews." They hurled blasphemies and insults on Him.

Once Jesus gave up His spirit, there was an earthquake and the curtain at the entrance to the Holy of Holies in the temple was split in two from the top to the bottom.

Signs, indeed.

But perhaps the greatest irony was what was said by the Roman centurion who had watched the entire event: "Surely this man was the Son of God!" (Mark 15:39).

Much debate continues to exist regarding the definitive spot where Jesus was crucified—known as Golgotha—and the location of the actual tomb where Jesus was buried and resurrected on the third day. Most biblical scholars believe that the Tomb of the Holy Sepulcher is where Jesus was crucified and that He was buried close by. Others, a much smaller group, believe that the Garden Tomb was the true burial site of Jesus.

I personally have no way of knowing the truth, but I must say that when I am at the Garden Tomb, I feel deeper in my spirit His very presence.

It doesn't ultimately matter where it happened. It matters that it *did* happen!

If you visit Rome today, you will no doubt want to explore the Coliseum, built during AD 70–80. This is the largest amphitheater in the Roman world and was constructed in large part with the spoils of war after the destruction of Jerusalem and the Jewish revolt in AD 70. Even now you can still see the Titus Arch (named after the general who conquered the land), a menorah, and the trumpets and the table representing the conquered Jewish state.

The Coliseum in Rome was built to honor Caesar and the Roman kingdom, which appeared to be the most powerful "god" at the time. But the true Kingdom, and the true King, are alive and well all over the world today. The True Triumph.

Come . . . to Golgotha!

MY BROTHER: THE JEWISH BAPTIST PREACHER

Far from the land of Israel, on an island called Manhattan, stands a beautiful, historic church on 57th Street, across from Carnegie Hall. Many visitors to New York City who pass by this church are surprised to see this plaque next to its doors:

CALVARY BAPTIST CHURCH, 1847
Reverend David Epstein, Senior Pastor

Many think, "Am I seeing things? A Reverend *Epstein* of a *Baptist* church?"

Yes. My brother, Dave, is indeed the pastor of this wonderful church and has been for the last twenty years. When I told him about this book, he was quick to understand my desire to get people to truly dig deep into the greater meaning of the Scriptures.

I was delighted when he agreed to make this contribution to our efforts with insights on two of the most important Scripture readings related to our Lord's sacrifice and what it really means for us.

FATHER FORGIVE THEM . . . (LUKE 23:32–43)
By David Epstein

In Luke 23 we have the graphic story of three dead men walking: Jesus and two robbers, all condemned to death and executed together. What's so interesting is that, according to the accounts in Matthew and Mark, everyone was mocking and cursing Jesus, including the two criminals—and then Luke gives us the rest of the story.

Suddenly, around noon, three hours into the crucifixions, one robber had a change of heart. He rebuked his partner in crime, acknowledging his own guilt and the innocence of Jesus. More, he asked Jesus to "remember me when you come into your kingdom" (v. 42).

What happened? What led to this man's transformation? Jesus made seven statements while on the cross for six hours—but the only thing He said for the first three hours between 9:00 a.m. and noon was, "Father, forgive them, for they do not know what they are doing" (v. 34). The grammar indicates that Jesus offered this prayer for forgiveness more than once. The imperfect active indicative translated in most versions as "Jesus said" actually indicates more continuous or repeated action, not a onetime statement. The biblical Greek word ἔλεγεν literally means "He was saying"; therefore, this prayer for forgiveness was the recurring theme for three hours.

The only way to understand one man's transformation is by the amazing power of forgiveness—God's love. The result was: "Remember me." And the response of Jesus was: "Truly I tell you, today you will be with me in paradise" (v. 43).

So why did one man embrace forgiveness and the other refuse it? Only God knows. The real question is: *Which of the two are you?*

THEY SHALL NEVER PERISH . . . (JOHN 10:27–30)

By David Epstein

Everything we love the most in life can be lost. Does that include salvation itself? Can we lose God's love? In John 10:28, Jesus, while describing Himself as the Good Shepherd who loves and sacrifices His life for His sheep, declared: "I give them eternal life, and they shall never perish." How strong is this promise?

In biblical Greek, the strongest negative that exists is called emphatic negation. It occurs when the negative particle of the indicative mood, ου, in concert with the negative particle of the non-indicative mood, μη, is joined to the verb—in this case, απολωνται, which means "to perish" or "to be destroyed."

What Jesus means is this: Those who genuinely believe in Him will never lose His love—they are saved and secure forever. No one who follows Him will ever, under any circumstances, for any reason, perish. Jesus isn't a liar. His death was not in vain ("the Good Shepherd gives His life for the sheep"), His promise is not in doubt ("they shall never perish"), and His power is not in question ("no one will snatch them out of my hand" or "my Father's hand"—a two-fisted salvation).

Therefore, salvation is not just a gift that God gives to us, which is wonderful enough, but we are a gift exchanged between the Father and the Son. Salvation is not just something that belongs to us; more importantly, we belong to Him. When will the Father take back the gift He gave to His Son? When will the Son take back the gift He gave to His Father? *Never!*[1]

When Jesus went to the cross, He didn't say, "Father, I hope this works." He said, "It is finished." That phrase, τετέλεσται, is a biblical Greek word signifying a completed action in the past, on the cross, with continuing life-changing consequences in the present. It means paid in full. Mission accomplished. You can go to the bank on it!

Jesus didn't die on Good Friday so the whole world *might* get saved, only to get lost again. Jesus died on Good Friday so the whole church *would* get saved—and stay saved forever. There is no "maybe," or "hope so," or "might be" in the death of Jesus. There is only "yes" and "know so" and "shall be."[2]

MORE FROM RABBI JASON

GOLGOTHA, THE CRUCIFIXION, AND ADAM

Have you ever wondered why Jesus had to die on a cross? The answer given by most people is that this was a common means of execution by the Romans. But surely something as important as the death of God's Son was not based solely upon Rome's proclivity for brutal means of execution like crucifixion. There must be something more.

How did sin enter the world? The first man and woman took from the tree of the knowledge of good and evil, and they ate the one thing in the garden of Eden that the Lord had prohibited (Genesis 3:6). Their disobedience led to the fall and their exile from Eden.

Redemption required a repair (*tikkun*, in Hebrew) for their sin. The first man and woman could not correct what they had done. What did God do? Since sin entered by means of a tree, God put His Son on a tree, in the form of a cross, to redeem us from the sin of the first man and woman. The Lord put Jesus, the second Adam, back on the tree for you and me to restore and make restitution for what had been stolen from the tree in the garden.

The first Adam brought death by means of a tree, but the second Adam brought life by means of His death on one! Concerning this, the apostle Paul wrote: "For since death came through a man, the resurrection of the dead also has come through a Man. For as in Adam all die, so also in Messiah will all be made alive. But each in its own order: Messiah the firstfruits; then, at His coming, those who belong to Messiah" (1 Corinthians 15:21–23 TLV).

Thank God for the tree, for it is the means by which the Lord sets us free and makes eternal life possible.

As always, there is even more. As Jesus hung on the cross, He had a crown of thorns on His head. Have you ever wondered why? The Roman soldiers put a crown of thorns on His head to mock His claim to be King Messiah. But the deeper spiritual reason for the crown of thorns also ties back to the garden of Eden. The sign of the curse of creation was that the ground would "produce thorns and thistles" (Genesis 3:18). By wearing a crown of thorns at His crucifixion, Jesus, the second Adam, took upon Himself the curse of creation, to undo it for the purpose of restoring the blessing!

Not only was Jesus' head pierced, but His hands, feet, and side were pierced as well. His hands were pierced, for it was with human hands that Adam and Eve stole from the tree. His side was pierced, because it was Eve, the one taken from Adam's side, who led Adam into temptation—I believe that by having His side pierced, Jesus was making atonement for the woman's role in the fall. Finally, Jesus' feet were pierced, because the first messianic prophecy states that the seed of the woman, meaning the messianic seed, would come and crush the head of the serpent, as stated in Genesis 3:14–15:

> ADONAI *Elohim* said to the serpent, "Because you did this,
> Cursed are you above all the livestock
> and above every animal of the field.
> On your belly will you go,
> and dust will you eat
> all the days of your life.
> I will put animosity
> between you and the woman—
> between your seed and her seed.
> He will crush your head,
> and you will crush his heel." (TLV)

Messiah's hands and feet were pierced so that He might overcome sin, Satan, and death for our sake. And Jesus wearing the crown of thorns demonstrates that He loved us so much that He was willing to identify with our pain and suffering and taste death so that we might experience life!

CHAPTER 23

JERUSALEM

The Jewish Festivals

The LORD said to Moses, "Speak to the Israelites and say to them: 'These are my appointed festivals, the appointed festivals of the LORD, which you are to proclaim as sacred assemblies.'"

—LEVITICUS 23:1–2

I think if you ask most believers if they have ever heard that everything important in Jesus' life took place during one of the traditional Jewish festivals, they would probably say no. Most wouldn't even be able to list the Jewish festivals, much less describe the importance of them in Jewish life. This is typical of the problem we are up against as we try to educate Christians regarding the foundations of our faith. Perhaps if we could learn how important Jesus felt these festivals were, we might grow to understand how important they should be to us as believers.

The city of Jerusalem is an integral part of these Jewish festivals. The Lord declared, "I have chosen Jerusalem for my Name to be there" (2 Chronicles 6:6). Thus, Jerusalem became the spiritual center of Israel, the place where God would place His name, causing His presence to dwell in the temple. Jerusalem was the place of pilgrimage, for everyone in Israel was commanded by God to appear before Him three times a year—during the three pilgrimage festivals of Passover, Pentecost, and Tabernacles—to offer sacrifices and firstfruit offerings in the temple.

Understanding the setting and celebration of these Jewish festivals brings new light to familiar stories of Jesus' life. For example, Jason explained to me during our first meeting in December 2016 that on the night that Jesus was born, the shepherds in the fields and the sheep they were tending were not ordinary sheep or shepherds. (He mentioned these truths earlier in this book, but they are worth repeating.)

The Bible is clear that the land directly surrounding Jerusalem was controlled by the Levitical priests, and everything either grown, raised, or born in that area was for one purpose: to be sacrificed on the altar of God in the temple of God for the people of God. Bethlehem is only three miles away from Jerusalem.

When we understand the Jewish feast of Passover, we realize the sheep that the shepherds were tending were born for the same reason that Jesus was born: to die for the forgiveness of sins! And just as Jesus was perfect, these lambs raised to be Passover sacrifices had to be perfect, too, without any defect or blemish. Do you know what shepherds in Bethlehem used to do to assure a sheep's perfection when it was first born? They wrapped the newborn lamb in swaddling cloths and laid it in a manger!

When the angel explained this sign to the Levitical shepherds, they would have understood the significance of finding the newborn baby wrapped in swaddling cloths and lying in a manger, because they knew that this baby was holy—set apart for sacred use—and in fact, this baby would be "the Lamb of God, who takes away the sin of the world!" (John 1:29), as John the Baptist later described Him.

Do you see how understanding the Jewish feasts can shed new light on the Scripture? If you don't have goose bumps right now, I haven't done a very good job of explaining this!

As Rabbi Jason explains next, every major event in Jesus' life happened on a Jewish holiday.

Come . . . to Jerusalem!

More from Rabbi Jason

An Overview of God's Appointed Feasts

Every follower of Jesus should be interested in the biblical holidays because Jesus Himself celebrated the Jewish festivals! More importantly, every major event in Jesus' life occurred on one of these Jewish holidays. For instance, Jesus is said to have been born around the time of Sukkot, the festival that focuses on God's presence, provision, and protection. Jesus' death was on Passover, the holiday that promises redemption. As we saw in chapter 19, the Last Supper of our Lord was a Passover Seder.

The biblical holidays are part of the inheritance of all followers of Messiah. Understanding the holidays gives us a deeper understanding and greater insight into the person and work of Jesus. Since much of Jesus' life and ministry revolved around the Jewish festivals, a fuller revelation of Jesus can be ours when we grasp the significance of these appointed times.

On the lighter side, as you study the Jewish feasts, you will find that our God is not merely about fasting; He is also very fond of feasting. He is a God of celebration. He wants you to come and join His party. Now let's take a moment to briefly explore the spiritual meaning and transformative nature of these biblical holidays.

Leviticus 23 describes the calendar of yearly feasts for God's people, breaking them into three cycles. The weekly celebration of the Sabbath (*Shabbat*, in Hebrew) is the first holiday mentioned. This Hebrew word means "rest." God rested on the seventh day and commanded Israel to do the same in the Ten Commandments (Exodus 20:8). From the days of Moses to the present, the Jewish people have celebrated the *Shabbat* starting at sundown on Friday and ending at sundown on Saturday. God rested on the seventh day, so we do as He did.

The spring holidays are Passover, Firstfruits, and Pentecost. These are holidays that reflect God's work of the past and were fulfilled in the first coming of Messiah. If you're scratching your head, let me explain briefly.

PASSOVER AND REDEMPTION

The focus of Passover (*Pesach*, in Hebrew) is redemption, which leads to freedom. The Lord redeemed the Israelites from Egypt, freeing them from the bondage of slavery. Centuries later, Jesus (*Yeshua*, in Hebrew) died as the Passover Lamb to redeem us from death and break the bondage of sin. Redemption in the days of Moses was meant to mirror the future redemption through the death of Messiah. Jesus is the ultimate fulfillment of the promise of redemption.

THE FEAST OF FIRSTFRUITS AND THE RESURRECTION

During the celebration of Firstfruits (*Yom HaBikkurim*, in Hebrew), the focus is resurrection. This was an agricultural holiday that celebrated the firstfruits of the harvest, which were brought from the fields to the temple on the second day of Passover. Fittingly, thousands of years later, Jesus was brought back from the dead during this festival. In 1 Corinthians 15:20, Paul tells us, "But now Messiah has been raised from the dead, the firstfruits of those who have fallen asleep" (TLV). Though Jesus fulfilled the promise of this holiday in His resurrection, there is also a prophetic fulfillment of this feast in which the firstfruits of the harvest symbolize the future resurrection of believers at the end of the age.

Pentecost, Sinai, and the Gift of the Holy Spirit

The Feast of Pentecost (*Shavuot*, in Hebrew) focuses on revelation. This holiday commemorates the giving of the Torah to Moses on Mount Sinai. During Jesus' time on earth, He gave the Holy Spirit to the disciples in Jerusalem on Pentecost. There is something significant about the fact that God chose the same day, both in the Old Testament and New Testament, to give the gift of Word and Spirit. In Genesis 1, the Spirit hovered over the formless surface of the watery earth, then God spoke the words, "Let there be light," and there was light (Genesis 1:3). Word and Spirit combined to bring about new creation and greater revelation.

During His lifetime, Jesus fulfilled the focus and promise of all three spring holidays—redemption, resurrection, and revelation.

The Feast of Trumpets and the Return of Messiah

The fall holidays are *Rosh Hashanah* (Feast of Trumpets), *Yom Kippur* (Day of Atonement), and *Sukkot* (Feast of Tabernacles). These holidays are awaiting their prophetic future fulfillment.

Rosh Hashanah (Feast of Trumpets) is the Jewish New Year and is "trumpeted in" with the blowing of the *shofar* (a ram's horn). This holiday points to repentance (changing one's way of thinking and being), resolving to make a better life, and ideally returning or regathering to God. At the sound of the *shofar* in a day yet to come, God will gather all His people from the four corners of the earth to Himself at the return of Messiah (Isaiah 27:13; 1 Corinthians 15:52; 1 Thessalonians 4:16).

The Day of Atonement and the Redemption of Israel

Yom Kippur means "atonement," or to repair a wrong so that we can be one with the Holy One. (Notice the word *atonement* can be broken down as at-one-ment.) This feast also focuses on repentance and redemption and forgiveness from the sins of the previous year. In the future fulfillment of this holiday, all Israel, as well as all the nations, will look upon the One they pierced and recognize Him as the Messiah (Zechariah 12:10). This will result in the fullness of redemption being realized. In Jewish thought, this is the final redemption.

The Feast of Tabernacles and the Messianic Kingdom

Sukkot (Feast of Tabernacles) is a time for rejoicing. This holiday commemorates the wandering of the Israelites in the desert. The shelters (*sukkot*, in Hebrew) relate to the temporary structures in which they lived as they wandered. This holiday commemorates how God provided manna from heaven to feed them, water from the stones to quench them, and a pillar of cloud by day and fire by night to guide them. Ultimately, it reflects God's presence, provision, and protection. Many Messianic Jews believe that Jesus was born during this holiday. When the future promise of Sukkot is fulfilled, the kingdom of God will be established, and we will all rejoice. According to the prophet Zechariah, all the nations of the world will join the Jewish people in

Jerusalem to celebrate the Feast of Tabernacles. "Then all the survivors from all the nations that attacked Jerusalem will go up from year to year to worship the King, ADONAI-Tzva'ot, and to celebrate Sukkot" (Zechariah 14:16 TLV).

In addition to the fall and spring holidays, which are known as the major holidays and are found in Leviticus 23, there are two other minor but key Jewish holidays mentioned in Scripture: Purim and Hanukkah.

THE FEAST OF PURIM, ESTHER, AND THE PROVIDENCE OF GOD

Purim is found in the book of Esther. Intrigue, sabotage, fear, courage, romance, and rising to one's destiny may sound like a soap opera, but the story of Esther is a chronicled struggle between good and evil, where the hidden hand of God isn't seen but is at work on behalf of His people. The story of Esther and the celebration of Purim is ultimately about God working all things together for the good (Romans 8:28). At Purim, we realize that when we cannot see the providential hand of God, we must trust the heart of God. Realizing the goodness of the Father stirs us to rejoice!

THE FEAST OF DEDICATION AND THE LIGHT OF THE WORLD

Hanukkah is the Feast of Dedication found in both the book of Daniel and the gospel of John. It commemorates the miraculous rededication of the temple in Jerusalem after it was defiled by the Greeks. It honors and celebrates the miracles God did, such as one night's *cruse* (jug) of oil for the menorah providing eight nights' worth of light and the victory of the outnumbered Israelites over the Greeks. God delivered the many into the hands of the few, proving Zechariah 4:6, which declares, "'Not by might nor by power, but by my Spirit,' says the LORD Almighty." Some believe that Jesus called Himself "the light of the world" in John

8:12 during Hanukkah, while others believe He made this statement during Sukkot. In John 10, Jesus went up to Jerusalem with His disciples to celebrate the Feast of Dedication. This holiday's prophetic fulfillment will occur when the light of the Messiah shines forth to all the ends of the world and we become the light that God calls us to be.

Why is learning about these Jewish festivals so important? It is in looking back at what God has done that we can see forward to His future plans for us. "'For I know the plans I have for you,' declares the LORD, 'plans to prosper you and not to harm you, plans to give you hope and a future'" (Jeremiah 29:11).

CHAPTER 24

THE UPPER ROOM AND TEMPLE COURTS

Pentecost Sunday

*When the day of Pentecost came, they were all together in
one place. Suddenly a sound like the blowing of a violent
wind came from heaven and filled the whole house where
they were sitting. They saw what seemed to be tongues of
fire that separated and came to rest on each of them.*

—ACTS 2:1–3

During our first Rock and Road Experience tour with Ray, he
explained to us that two important events occurred in Acts
2:1–3. The first thing that happened is the Holy Spirit entered the
room and rested on all the believers there. The second is that the
disciples traveled a short way to the steps leading up to the temple.

Come . . . to the Upper Room!

MORE FROM RABBI JASON

THE UPPER ROOM, PENTECOST, AND SINAI REVISITED

The Upper Room was not only the place of the Last Supper, but it was also where the disciples prepared themselves to receive the gift of the Holy Spirit on Pentecost (Acts 2).

It is impossible to fully grasp the outpouring of God's Spirit (and what is commonly understood as the birth of the church) without first understanding the biblical roots of Pentecost. *Pentecost*, which means "Fifty Days," is the Greek term for the biblical Jewish holiday known as *Shavuot*, the Feast of Weeks (Exodus 34:22; Leviticus 23:9–22; Deuteronomy 16:10).

God commanded Israel upon entering the Promised Land to count seven complete weeks, starting on the second day of Passover, and on the fiftieth day to celebrate *Shavuot/Pentecost. Shavuot* in part was an agricultural holiday that began on the second day of Passover with the offering of the firstfruits of the barley harvest and culminated fifty days later with the offering of the firstfruits of the wheat harvest.

Jesus died on Passover. He also rose from the dead on the holiday called Firstfruits (*Yom HaBikkurim*), which was an agricultural holiday that took place on the second day of Passover. In ancient times, an offering of the firstfruits of the barley harvest was given to the Lord. It would be waved before the Lord as a sign of thanksgiving and in eager expectation of greater blessing to come. If you had a good early harvest, it was a guarantee that you would also have an abundant later harvest. Not only were the firstfruits a sign of the greater harvest to come, but the feast started the forty-nine-day countdown to Shavuot/Pentecost.

Nothing is random with God. Therefore, it is appropriate that Jesus, who died on Passover, would arise from the dead as "the firstfruits of those who have fallen asleep" (1 Corinthians 15:20). After He rose, He instructed the disciples to "not leave Jerusalem, but wait for the gift my Father promised. . . . For John baptized with water, but in a few days you will be baptized with the Holy Spirit" (Acts 1:4–5). Jesus' resurrection on the Feast of Firstfruits started the countdown to Pentecost, which was His Father's gift—the biggest biblical God party on record, where God literally rocked the house, and there were three thousand salvations in one day! Jesus not only died as the Passover Lamb but was raised from the dead on the day the firstfruits of the barley were offered in the temple!

Why did Jesus choose Pentecost Sunday as the day to pour out the Holy Spirit? To understand this question, one must know the key historical event that happened on this day. It was on the fiftieth day of Israel's coming out of Egypt that the Lord descended upon Mount Sinai and spoke the Ten Commandments to Israel. Thus, Shavuot is also known as *Zeman Mattan Torateinu*, or "the Time of the Giving of the Torah."

It is critical to understand that the Torah and the Spirit were given on the same day, the fiftieth day. But why is this so important? At the start of creation, "The earth was chaos and waste, darkness was on the surface of the deep, and the *Ruach Elohim* [Spirit of God] was hovering upon the surface of the water. Then God said, 'Let there be light!' and there was light" (Genesis 1:2–3 TLV). How does the Lord bring life out of the chaos and the darkness? By His Word and Spirit! In the same way that the original creation was birthed through Word and Spirit, the work of the new creation begins by God giving His Word and climaxes in the giving of His Spirit on the exact same calendar day so that we might experience the life and light of God's transforming power!

But there is still more! On the Day of Pentecost in the New

Testament, "a sound like the blowing of a violent wind came from heaven and filled the whole house where they were sitting. They saw what seemed to be tongues of fire that separated and came to rest on each of them. All of them were filled with the Holy Spirit and began to speak in other tongues as the Spirit enabled them" (Acts 2:2–4).

From a Jewish perspective, Acts 2 is considered to be a reenactment of Mount Sinai or, better yet, a second Sinai experience. The booming of the wind was like the thunderings at Sinai, and the tongues of fire over the disciples' heads were akin to the cleft tongue that came out of the mouth of God when He uttered the Ten Commandments. *Targum Neofiti*, an ancient Aramaic paraphrase of the Hebrew Bible, describes the giving of the Ten Commandments by the mouth of God, "like torches of fire, a torch of fire to the right and a torch of flame to the left. It flew and winged swiftly in the air of the heavens and turned around and became visible in all the camps of Israel and . . . became engraved on the two tablets of the covenant."[1]

In Acts 2, God again imprinted His Word as He did on Sinai. This time the stone of Sinai was replaced as God wrote His new covenant: "I will make a new covenant with the people of Israel. . . . I will put my law in their minds and write it on their hearts" (Jeremiah 31:31, 33). God does not want His Word to remain written on stone tablets; He wants His words to be written on our hearts by the power of the Spirit!

As God redeemed Israel, He has redeemed us through Messiah, and by His power He is transforming all who believe into new creations with new identities and purpose. Israel was called a royal priesthood, a holy nation, on Mount Sinai. Peter declares the same for us:

> But you are a chosen people, a royal priesthood, a holy nation, God's special possession, that you may declare the praises of

him who called you out of darkness into his wonderful light. Once you were not a people, but now you are the people of God; once you had not received mercy, but now you have received mercy. (1 Peter 2:9–10)

Peter himself became a new creation during Pentecost. Instead of the cowering coward who denied Jesus three times, he became *Petra* (Peter), living up to the name Jesus gave him, which means "rock." Peter, filled with the power of the Holy Spirit, preached his first sermon and birthed the early church during this Pentecost. Just as in Genesis, as the Spirit hovered over the deep, God spoke the Word, and creation occurred. As it was in the beginning, so it was on that Shavuot (Pentecost) in Jerusalem—the union of Word and Spirit swelled the ranks of the followers of Yeshua by three thousand new creations that day. Word and Spirit resulted in newness of life!

Remember, what God has done in the past, He wants to do again in the present and the future. The past is more than events that have already happened. Those events reflect the heart of God and what He desires to do in and through you. Seek the Lord for your own personal Pentecost as individuals and as a church, and watch the amazing work of transformation that comes through His Word and Spirit.

CHAPTER 25

THE TEMPLE MOUNT

The Spiritual Center of the World

I have chosen Jerusalem that My Name would abide there.
—2 CHRONICLES 6:6 TLV

The Temple Mount in Jerusalem is a deeply moving, almost otherworldly place to visit. I always have dual emotions when I enter the courtyard that leads to the Western Wall. I can't help but cry for all that was lost due to Israel's disobedience to God and His law, resulting in the numerous times that it was destroyed. And yet there were also those thrilling times when the people of Israel repented of their sins and asked for God's forgiveness. And God faithfully answered their prayers.

It's almost a metaphor for our own spiritual ups and downs. No doubt the Temple Mount is steeped in history and future end times significance.

Come . . . to the Temple Mount!

MORE FROM RABBI JASON

JERUSALEM, THE SPIRITUAL CENTER OF CREATION AND OUR FUTURE HOME

New York is known as the "city that never sleeps." There is a palpable energy to New York City that makes it unique. On a spiritual level, Jerusalem is similar. Jerusalem abounds with the palpable presence of God that makes the city spiritually electric. Just walking the streets of the Old City can be a spiritual experience. But what makes the city of Jerusalem so special and unique?

The uniqueness of Jerusalem can be attributed to the fact that it is the city chosen by God to be the spiritual center of Israel and ultimately the whole world. Concerning Jerusalem, the Lord declared, "I have chosen Jerusalem that My Name would abide there and I have chosen David to be over My people Israel" (2 Chronicles 6:6 TLV). Israel was chosen to be the political center but more importantly the spiritual center, the place where God would place His Name and cause His presence to dwell in the temple.

One of the primary reasons Jerusalem is the spiritual center of the world is the Temple Mount.

To better understand this, we must go back to the first book of the Bible. The father of faith and the first Hebrew patriarch was Abraham. Abraham went through ten trials of faith that demonstrated both his faithfulness and complete, loving devotion to the Creator of all. At his first trial, Abraham heard the divine command, "Get going out from your land, and from your relatives, and from your father's house, to the land that I will show you" (Genesis 12:1 TLV). At the tenth and final trial, Abraham heard similar words: "Take your son, your only son whom you love—Isaac—and go to the land of Moriah, and offer him there as a burnt offering on one of the mountains about which I will tell you" (Genesis 22:2 TLV).

To which mountain did the Lord lead Abraham? It was Mount Moriah in Jerusalem, the same mountain that the Lord chose for the site of the temple, His abode in this world. God is love (1 John 4:8), and Mount Moriah is the place where one of the first and greatest demonstrations of love for the Lord occurred through Abraham. Can there be any greater act of love than offering your beloved child who was born supernaturally in old age in fulfillment of the Lord's promise? Abraham was not just offering the one he most loved, but he was putting his entire future on that altar. What an act of radical love!

It was on this mountain that God's covenant was confirmed for the final time to Abraham, which caused the Lord to choose the summit of Mount Moriah as the site of the temple's Holy of Holies, the ultimate embodiment of the relationship between God and His people, Israel. Mount Moriah is the location where Abraham demonstrated his great love for God and the place where the first commandment was most tangibly demonstrated for the first time! This is also the place where Abraham met and paid tithes to Melchizedek, the king of the city of Salem.

The site of Mount Moriah was also significant for King David. In 2 Samuel 24, Satan incited King David to take a census of the people. When David realized that his decision to number the people was sinful in the sight of God, he turned to the Lord and prayed to be forgiven. In response, the Lord sent the prophet Gad to King David. Gad told David that he must choose one of the following punishments: either seven years of famine, three months of running from his adversaries who would seek his life, or three days of pestilence from the Angel of the Lord (2 Samuel 24:11–13).

David chose the third of these three options, declaring that he would rather "fall into the hands of the LORD, for his mercy is very great" (1 Chronicles 21:13). As a result, God sent an angel to bring a plague throughout the land. Upon reaching Jerusalem, the Lord commanded the angel to desist. As the angel of the Lord stood by the threshing floor of Ornan the Jebusite on Mount Moriah, David's eyes perceived this angel "standing between heaven and earth, with a drawn sword in his hand extended over Jerusalem" (v. 16). The angel then commanded David through the prophet Gad to build an altar to the Lord on this site. This is believed to be the very same site at which Abraham offered Isaac and encountered the Lord! This was the site of Solomon's temple, the very place where the presence of God dwelled among His people.

Even in Babylonian exile, after the temple was destroyed, Daniel prayed three times a day toward the Temple Mount in Jerusalem at the time the daily sacrifices should have been offered.

In 538 BC, Zerubbabel, the leader of the tribe of Judah, returned as part of the first wave of exiles who came back to Jerusalem (Ezra 1:1–2). By command of the Persian king Cyrus, Zerubbabel, who was appointed as the governor of Judah, began to rebuild the temple with the assistance of the high priest Joshua (Ezra 3:2–3, 8). It took several years to rebuild the temple's foundation, and construction was delayed due to hostility from the Samaritans (Ezra 4:1–5). Because of this political opposition, the work of the temple was stopped for seventeen years (Ezra 4:21). Through the support of Ezra and the prophetic encouragement of Zechariah and Haggai, Zerubbabel resumed the work on the temple. After several years of construction, in 516 BC the temple was finally finished and dedicated with great joy (Ezra 6:16).

The temple built by Zerubbabel is often referred to as the Second Temple.

Upon seeing the Second Temple, some of the Jewish returnees from Babylonian exile felt a tremendous sense of disappointment. In their eyes, it fell far short of the beauty and glory of Solomon's temple. It was much smaller, less ornate, did not house the ark of the covenant, and its dedication was not accompanied by any miracles such as the presence of God consuming the sacrifices on the altar.

Even though all the above was true, the Lord spoke through the prophet Haggai, saying, "'The glory of this latter House will be greater than the former,' says *ADONAI-Tzva'ot*. 'In this place, I will grant *shalom*'—it is a declaration of *ADONAI-Tzva'ot*" (Haggai 2:9 TLV). How was this fulfilled? God used Herod the Great to bring this prophecy to pass. Herod began a large-scale renovation of the temple and expansion of the Temple Mount. The work on the Second Temple was one of the largest construction projects of the first century BC. Because of the immense resources Herod invested, the Second Temple became one of the wonders of the ancient world. Herod's motivation, according to the historian Josephus, was to make a name and legacy for himself—but God used this ambition to fulfill His promise made through Haggai about the glory of the latter House (Haggai 2:3–9). This is a great reminder that God can use anyone, even if they are not aware of it, to fulfill His plans and purposes. The Second Temple stood on the Temple Mount from 516 BC until AD 70, when it was destroyed by the Romans.

Like Daniel did when he was in exile, traditional Jews still pray toward the Temple Mount in Jerusalem. It was and always will be the holiest site and the place of the Lord's abode. Jews pray at the Western Wall (*kotel*, in Hebrew) for this reason. The Western Wall is the only remaining wall of the Temple Mount, so the Western Wall remains are holy ground due to their proximity to the Holy of Holies.

But of course there is more! Song of Solomon 2:9 states: "Look! He is standing behind our wall—gazing through the windows, peering through the lattice" (TLV). Many Jewish rabbis interpret "our wall" in this verse as referring to the Western Wall. The reason is that the Hebrew word for "wall" in this passage is *kotel*, the Hebrew name for the Western Wall.

Song of Solomon 2:9 is also seen as connected to another promise that the Lord made to King Solomon in 1 Kings 9:3: "The LORD said to him: 'I have heard the prayer and plea you have made before me; I have consecrated this temple, which you have built, by putting my Name there forever. My eyes and my heart will always be there.'" These verses are a promise that the Western Wall will never be destroyed because the Lord keeps watch over it in perpetuity.

The Zohar, a mystical commentary on the Torah, takes it a step further, explaining that the Hebrew word *kotel* can be broken into two parts, *ko* and *tel*. The letter *ko* has the numerical value of twenty-six, which is the same as the tetragrammaton (הוהי), the four letters in Hebrew that are often translated into English as YHVH or Yahweh. *Tel* is Hebrew for "hill." Thus, the name *kotel* is meant to allude to the fact that God's presence will always dwell on the Mount of God at the Western Wall.

For two thousand years, the Jewish people have mourned the destruction of the Second Temple. Each year, on the ninth day of the Hebrew month of Av (the day the temple was destroyed in AD 70), observant Jews fast, mourn, and pray for the rebuilding of the temple in Jerusalem. But why would the Lord allow the temple to be destroyed? The choice of the location for the temple was connected to—and symbolic of—its spiritual foundation, which was love. The First Temple was destroyed because of idolatry, and the Second Temple was destroyed due to a senseless hatred that Jewish people had toward one another.

Thus, the First Temple was destroyed when Israel broke the first and greatest commandment, which is, "Love the LORD your God with all your heart and with all your soul and with all your strength" (Deuteronomy 6:5). The Second Temple was destroyed when Israel broke the second greatest commandment, which is, "Love your neighbor as yourself" (Leviticus 19:18).

When love was lost, God's house crumbled because its foundation was destroyed! Jesus came proclaiming and embodying the love of God. He offered the cure that could have prevented the temple's destruction as well as the painful tragedy of exile that resulted and continues to this day.

Love builds; hate destroys. The questions we must ask ourselves as we reflect on the reason for the destruction of the temple are: "Have I learned lessons of love?" and "Whom am I harboring hate and offense in my heart toward?" Hatred and offense build fences that block us from having a real, meaningful connection to God and others. If we harbor offense and bitterness in our hearts, then we are also guilty of contributing to the destruction of God's house, the temple. But if we come in the opposite spirit, one of gratuitous radical love, then we are helping to pave the way for the return of Jesus and the restoration of God's temple in Jerusalem, a place of worship for Israel and the nations!

Clearly, the Temple Mount is important to the Jewish people. But how important should it be for Christians? I believe this is an important question to answer.

On at least three occasions, Jesus lamented over Jerusalem. Jesus even wept over the impending destruction of Jerusalem because of their senseless hostility and rejection of Him as their Messiah:

As He drew near and saw Jerusalem, He wept over her, saying, "If only you had recognized this day the things that lead to *shalom*! But now they are hidden from your eyes. For the days will come upon you when your enemies will surround you with barricades and hem you in on all sides. And they will smash you to the ground—you and your children within you. And they won't leave within you one stone upon another, because you did not recognize the time of your visitation." (Luke 19:41–44 TLV)

If Jesus was saddened over Jerusalem's fate, should we not be as well? Should not those who call themselves His disciples also care for Jerusalem and the Jewish people? As the psalmist exhorted, "Pray for the peace of Jerusalem: 'May they prosper who love you'" (Psalm 122:6 NASB). This promise of prosperity is rooted in the promise that God made to Abraham concerning his descendants: "I will bless those who bless you, and the one who curses you I will curse. And in you all the families of the earth will be blessed" (Genesis 12:3 NASB). Praying for Jerusalem and the Jewish people is one way to bless Israel and experience the promise that is attached to it.

By praying for Jerusalem and the Jewish people, we are not just demonstrating concern for the city that the Lord loves, but also our desire to see His kingdom come on earth as it is in heaven. The final redemption of the world is dependent upon Israel's acceptance of Jesus as King Messiah:

O Jerusalem, Jerusalem who kills the prophets and stones those sent to her! How often I longed to gather your children together, as a hen gathers her chicks under her wings, but you were not willing. Look, your house is left to you desolate! For I tell you, you will never see Me until you say, "*Baruch ha-ba b'shem* ADONAI. Blessed is He who comes in the name of the LORD!" (Luke 13:34–35 TLV)

The phrase Jesus uses, "*Baruch ha-ba,*" is a common Hebrew expression of welcome used to greet the groom as he walks down the aisle, and it is used on doormats of Jewish homes in Israel. Until the Jews, as a whole, welcome Jesus as Redeemer and Son of David, the messianic kingdom will not be established on earth.

And what is the name of this home? The apostle John answered this for us: "I also saw the holy city—the New Jerusalem—coming down out of heaven from God, prepared as a bride adorned for her husband" (Revelation 21:2 TLV). It is to this New Jerusalem that all believers will regularly make the pilgrimage:

Then all the survivors from all the nations that attacked Jerusalem will go up from year to year to worship the King, ADONAI-*Tzva'ot,* and to celebrate *Sukkot.* Furthermore, if any of the nations on earth do not go up to Jerusalem to worship the King, ADONAI-*Tzva'ot,* they will have no rain. (Zechariah 14:16–17 TLV)

"Then they will bring all your kinsmen from all the nations, as an offering to ADONAI, on horses and in chariots, and on litters, mules and camels, to My holy mountain Jerusalem," says ADONAI, "just as *Bnei-Yisrael* bring their grain offering in a clean vessel to the House of ADONAI. I will also take some of them as priests and for Levites," says ADONAI.

"For just as the new heavens and the new earth, which

I will make, will endure before Me"—it is a declaration of
ADONAI—"so your descendants and your name will endure."
(Isaiah 66:20–22 TLV)

In other words, Jerusalem was not just the home of David, the prophets, and the Jewish people, but is destined to become your home as well. In that day, Jerusalem will be a "house of prayer for all nations" and will fulfill its ultimate destiny to be the spiritual center of God's kingdom! It was the place of His Father's house! His Father is our Father, so we will all one day go up to Jerusalem to worship and rejoice with the Lord in the New Jerusalem! As we say at the end of every Passover Seder, "Next Year in Jerusalem" or, better yet, "the New Jerusalem!" May we all have the same heart for this amazing city and the Promised Land as David and the Son of David, Jesus!

Should we not take seriously the command to pray for the peace of Jerusalem and seek its well-being? All who pray for the peace of Jerusalem will prosper.

CHAPTER 26

THE DEAD SEA

"The Waters Shall Be Healed"

*Moreover, in that day living waters will flow from
Jerusalem, half toward the eastern sea and half toward the
western sea, both in the summer and in the winter.*

—ZECHARIAH 14:8 TLV

The Dead Sea is one of the most extraordinary places in the
world. It is more than four hundred meters below sea level and
is considered the lowest point on dry land on planet Earth.

The water in the Dead Sea is almost ten times saltier than the
ocean, making it completely inhospitable to any life form. Tourists
flock to this site to enjoy the phenomenon of buoyantly floating
on the surface, completely incapable of sinking in the hypersaline
water. The beauty treatments made from the various rich minerals

in the region are legendary, and it's not uncommon to watch a sea full of people floating and laughing with their faces covered in Dead Sea mud masques.

We are told by the experts that the water level of the Dead Sea has been receding at the alarming rate of one meter a year because of water being diverted from the Jordan River for agricultural purposes and the natural evaporation caused by the sea's own mineral works.

Gazing on the area now, it's almost impossible to believe that it was once a rich, fertile landscape—so inviting, in fact, that Abraham's nephew Lot chose it from all the land as far as his eye could see. Scripture tells us, "Lot looked around and saw that the whole plain of the Jordan toward Zoar was well watered, like the garden of the LORD, like the land of Egypt" (Genesis 13:10).

What? This devastated wilderness, this wasteland, was once a garden? How is that even possible? Well, the Scriptures give us a clue: "Then said he unto me: 'These waters issue forth toward the eastern region, and shall go down into the Arabah; and when they shall enter into the sea, into the sea of the putrid waters, the waters shall be healed. And it shall come to pass, that every living creature . . . shall live; and there shall be a very great multitude of fish . . . that all things be healed. . . .'" (Ezekiel 47:8–9 JPS Tanakh).[1]

A miracle is happening this very moment in the Dead Sea. Perhaps prophetic Scripture is even being fulfilled as recently as these past five years. A young tourist named Samantha Siegel discovered something extraordinary in the waters: freshwater ponds with actual fish and green plants along the shores! She took video of the fish swimming in the water,[2] and soon scientific experts and the naturally curious were on the scene to discover the truth.

A team of researchers from Ben Gurion University in the Negev Desert sent researchers to the floor of the Dead Sea. This had never been done before, because this super-saline environment renders regular scuba gear completely inoperable.

How they did it is not as important as what they found in 2011. The divers discovered huge craters on the seafloor, fifteen meters across and twenty meters deep, full of fresh fish and covered with mats full of microorganisms, with freshwater flowing from the craters![3]

While this discovery baffles the scientific world, it causes people of faith to rejoice. Much further research shall no doubt continue, but in the meantime, we believers can find encouragement in our walk with the Rabbi and gain strength from the Word of God, which never changes.

Come . . . to the Dead Sea!

CHAPTER 27

MASADA

The Jews' Last Stand against Rome

Live as free people.

—1 PETER 2:16

Masada is one of the most extraordinary sites in all of Israel. One of Herod's most architecturally astounding palaces, it sits directly next to the Dead Sea, just twelve miles east of Arad in the Negev Desert. The fortress of Masada was built between 37 and 31 BC, but it gained notoriety when it was besieged by the Roman Empire at the end of the first Jewish-Roman War. Approximately 960 Jewish rebels famously committed mass suicide rather than be overrun by the Roman legion.

In AD 73, the Roman governor Lucius Flavius Silva began building a siege ramp against the western face of the mountain to attack the Israelites. The ramp was completed in the spring, allowing the Romans to finally breach the wall of the fortress with a battering ram on April 16.

Originally, the Jewish rebels at the top of Masada threw stones at those building the ramp to fend off their enemies. To counter this tactic, the Romans made previously captured Jewish prisoners work at the forefront of the ramp. The Jewish rebels chose not to kill their fellow Jews, knowing full well it might mean their own demise.

When the Romans finally entered the fortress, they discovered that the Jewish defenders had set everything but the food storeroom on fire and had chosen to kill themselves rather than become Roman slaves. Apparently ten lots were drawn, and ten men were chosen as executioners; the rest lay down side by side and bared their necks. Finally, the last Jewish Zealot killed the remaining nine and then took his own life. The food was left untouched so the Romans would know without a doubt that the Jewish men, women, and children of Masada had not starved to death but had chosen freedom.[1]

By the way, the final day of the siege was the first day of Passover, the holiday on which the Jews celebrate their freedom from the bondage of slavery.

The lots have been discovered and can be seen today in the Israel Museum in Jerusalem. Eleven pottery shards have been excavated from the mountain. Each bears a name, including the name of the Zealot leader, Ben Yair.

We know most of these facts through the historical writings of Josephus, who had access to the Roman commanders at the time. Further testimony came from the only survivors of the Roman siege of Masada: two women and five children who had hidden during the final hours.[2]

Interestingly, coins have been found on the mountain that date all the way back to the Maccabean kings. And today, this is the site where the newest members of the Jewish army take their vows of allegiance to the state of Israel. Masada has become an eternal symbol of the Jewish fight for freedom.

Come . . . to Masada!

CHAPTER 28

THE QUMRAN CAVES

The Dead Sea Scrolls

*The grass withers and the flowers fall, but
the word of the Lord endures forever.*

—1 PETER 1:24–25

The Dead Sea Scrolls, one of history's greatest archaeological finds, were discovered between 1946 and 1947, just as the nation of Israel was being reestablished after ceasing to exist since the fall of Jerusalem to the Roman Empire in AD 70.

Talk about timing!

Some 981 ancient parchment scrolls were found in eleven caves along the northwest shore of the Dead Sea. This area is only thirteen miles east of Jerusalem, and as noted in chapter 26, it is 1,300 feet below sea level, making it the lowest point in the world.

Scholars have identified the remains of between 825 and 870 separate scrolls, and they can be divided into two categories: biblical and nonbiblical. Fragments of every book of the Old Testament except the book of Esther have been discovered, including nineteen copies of the book of Isaiah, twenty-five copies of Deuteronomy, and thirty copies of Psalms.

Interestingly, prophecies by Ezekiel, Jeremiah, and Daniel that are not included in the Bible were also written in the scrolls. And miraculously, the Isaiah scroll, found fundamentally intact, is one thousand years older than any previously known copy of the book of Isaiah.

Together, the Dead Sea Scrolls are the oldest group of Old Testament manuscripts ever found. And the way they were discovered was nothing short of miraculous.

Apparently a local Bedouin shepherd left his flock to look for a stray. As he searched, he came across a cave in the crevice on the mountainside. No one knows exactly why, but he threw a stone deep into the dark interior of the cave, only to be startled by the sound of shattered pots. When he entered the cave, he found a collection of large clay jars, most of them empty. But a few were intact and their lids were still tightly in place. When the shepherd looked further, he was disappointed at first to discover nothing in them but some old scrolls.

The truth is, this shepherd had stumbled upon one of the greatest archaeological discoveries of all time!

It is believed that the scrolls were originally written by a Jewish sect known as the Essenes sometime between 200 BC and AD 68. Though they are not mentioned by name in the New Testament, the Essenes were well documented by Josephus. They were a strict, Torah-believing, apocalyptic Jewish sect who felt that the religious leaders at the temple in Jerusalem were corrupt and had fallen away from the sacred text of Moses. They were led by a priest they called "The Teacher of Righteousness," who was opposed by the established religious leaders of the Pharisees and the Sadducees.[1]

The Essenes called themselves the "Sons of the Light," and they referred to their enemies as the "Sons of Darkness." Interestingly, they also called themselves "the poor" and members of "the Way" (the earliest name given to believers in Jesus). The Essenes believed the Holy Spirit dwelled within them, therefore they lived in "the house of holiness." Some experts believe that John the Baptist had at one time been a member of the Essene sect.

In addition to the Scripture scrolls, the Qumran caves housed many writings that were not Scripture. It's fascinating that certain biblical figures such as Abraham, Enoch, and Noah are mentioned in these additional scrolls, containing previously unknown stories about them. One scroll gives additional stories about Abraham and provides an alternate explanation of why God asked Abraham to sacrifice Isaac, his son! This Qumran text introduces a satanic figure called "Mastemah," who basically goads God into testing Abraham's faith, eerily reminiscent of Satan convincing God to test Job.[2] Numerous theories abound and are sure to be argued among scholars and laypeople alike for decades to come.

Of course, these additional sources are separate from Scripture. I just think it is interesting that they exist! These scrolls—though not Scripture—can shed extra light on the Scriptures themselves.

One of the most unusual of the Dead Sea Scrolls is the Copper Scroll, which records a list of sixty-four underground hiding places throughout Israel that are believed to be the locations of treasures from the temple in Jerusalem, hidden away for safekeeping.

Most curious is that, although the Qumran community existed during the time of Jesus' ministry, none of the scrolls mention Jesus or any of His followers by name. Regardless, the Dead Sea Scrolls reveal a community with many incredible parallels to the Jesus movement at the time. They prove that Christianity is rooted in Judaism, and the scrolls have been called "the evolutionary link" between Judaism and Christianity.

Come . . . to the Qumran Caves!

CHAPTER 29

TEL AVIV

The Mediterranean Capital of Cool

*"Your prayers and gifts to the poor have come up as a
memorial offering before God. Now send men to Joppa to
bring back a man named Simon who is called Peter. He is
staying with Simon the tanner, whose house is by the sea."*

—ACTS 10:4—6

When you visit the modern, sophisticated city of Tel Aviv, it's almost impossible to picture what it once was during biblical times. Today, Tel Aviv bustles with chic hotels, five-star restaurants, and boutiques and galleries selling the latest, hottest styles—all along the natural beauty of the Mediterranean Sea. The *New York Times* called Tel Aviv "the capital of Mediterranean cool."[1]

At times when I am in Tel Aviv, I almost feel as if I am in Santa Monica, California, because the resemblance is so extraordinary.

There's a common saying in Israel today: "Jerusalem prays; Tel Aviv plays." The contrast in the two very different cities is striking.

The small ancient village of Joppa, now known as Jaffa, still survives in Tel Aviv today. Though it is now a thriving, cultural oasis of restaurants and art galleries, it was once home to the oldest seaport in the world. It was also the home of Simon the tanner, where the apostle Peter received a crucial vision from God that completely transformed his faith (Acts 10:9–16). From this extraordinary experience, Peter set out to visit the home of Cornelius the centurion, just a short journey north in Caesarea Maritima, an event we looked at previously in chapter 9. There, Cornelius and his entire household heard Peter's testimony regarding Jesus the Messiah, and the Bible tells us every member was saved. This little, picturesque seaside port in Tel Aviv is the place where a miracle occurred in one Jewish man's heart, which, in turn, set off miracles in the hearts of millions of Gentiles worldwide.

Ironically, ancient Joppa is the same port that the prophet Jonah set out from centuries before in an attempt to flee from the Lord, who had told him to go to Nineveh, also to save the lives of non-Jewish sinners in desperate need of salvation. Jonah didn't want to go. Peter didn't want to go. You know what? Sometimes I don't want to go. But we are all called to get out of our biases and our preconceived ideas of what a ministry looks like and "Go into all the world and preach the Good News to everyone" (Mark 16:15 NLT).

Come . . . to Tel Aviv!

CONCLUSION

What Is Your Stone?

[David] took his staff in his hand, chose five smooth stones
from the stream, put them in the pouch of his shepherd's bag
and, with his sling in his hand, approached the Philistine.

—1 SAMUEL 17:40

I returned to the *Today Show* eight days after Frank passed into glory. My children, Cody and Cassidy, came to support me, standing in the wings. On that day, I felt the Lord leading me to share something deeper about Frank than most people knew. I had no idea what I was going to say, but I had a lifetime of experience of God's faithfulness to give me the words that He would want me to share.

I told the audience that, as a child, Frank had asked Jesus into his heart as Lord and Savior. He had considered himself a Christian his whole life. But he came to realize in the Holy Land that he actually had a religion all his life, but the joy resides in the *relationship* one has with our loving God, regardless of where or how often you go to church. This was profound for him—and life-changing.

At this writing, the video of that show, which went viral immediately, has reached over seventy million views.[1]

So even while we grieve losing our precious husband, father, and friend, we know that Frank Newton Gifford threw his last stone, bringing God's *shalom* to the chaos of the world.

What is your stone? What is your gift? How will you know it?

What is the one thing that you can do that no one else can do but you?

What is your stone?

GOING HOME

August 9, 2015

Precious in the sight of the LORD is the
death of his faithful servants.
—PSALM 116:15

August 9, 2015, dawned as a glorious, perfect summer Sunday. I was up early to help Cassidy get ready to leave for a flight to Santa Fe where she would begin a new film. I headed downstairs while it was still dark to let the dogs out, start the coffee, and begin my daily ritual of Scripture, prayer, and devotions while my husband, Frank, slept in upstairs. Two hours later, around 7:00 a.m., I heard the scale in Frank's bathroom declare: "Your weight is 178 pounds."

Perfect, I thought to myself. *It's going to be a good day. That's his favorite weight.*

Then Frank went about his typical morning routine: he showered, dressed in what he knew to be my favorite outfit of black jeans and a crisp white shirt, and came downstairs to pour his Dunkin

Donuts coffee and help himself to a big piece of cornbread while he opened his Bible on the big Restoration Hardware table and sat in his favorite chair, in his favorite room, in his favorite place in the world—our home in Connecticut on the Long Island Sound.

At 7:45 I saw him sitting there contentedly. As I climbed the steps to our bedroom, I told him, "I'm going to get ready for church, Frank Gifford." (I have always called him that since the day I met him.)

"Okay," he responded.

I took my time getting ready, finally heading down the staircase at 8:30, noticing the time and thinking, *Oh good, we've got an hour to have another cup of coffee before we need to leave for church.*

It's funny the things you remember.

As I descended, I looked into the sunroom, where I'd last seen him less than an hour before, but he wasn't seated at the table.

"Lamb?" I asked, thinking he might have stepped outside to watch the boats go by in the harbor.

I continued toward the sunroom and suddenly stopped in my tracks. There, on the floor just inside the sunroom, was my precious husband, lying on his back. The coffee cup had fallen, though not broken, and the coffee had spilled onto the floor.

I began to scream for help, knowing Cody was asleep on the second floor and our beloved friend Elvia Medina was in the kitchen.

Not knowing what else to do, I began to give Frank mouth-to-mouth resuscitation, praying all the while that Frank would come to, not knowing if he'd had a stroke or maybe choked on the cornbread.

Cody appeared and immediately began to give his father chest compressions, and Elvia ran to call 911. All I can remember clearly of these moments was the extraordinary, supernatural peace I was experiencing. I was able to rejoice at the same time I was trying to save Frank's life, just as Cody was. This is what the Bible calls the peace that passes all understanding (Philippians 4:7). I now know without a doubt that it is a real thing.

Finally, the EMTs arrived and confirmed to us what we already knew to be true: Frank was gone. One of them said to me after examining Frank: "Mrs. Gifford, I hope this comforts you. Your husband never knew he hit the ground." In other words, Frank never suffered.

I cried for joy hearing these words. They did comfort me, because it was an answer to prayer.

You see, my husband wasn't afraid of anything after the extraordinary life he had lived, except for one thing: he never wanted to be a burden on his family. He never wanted to be hooked up to machines or lose his dignity because of an illness.

"Please tell me if it ever gets to that, you'll pull the plug," he used to tell me.

"Honey," I'd answer each time, "I love you, but I'm not going to prison for you."

"Then trip over it!" he used to say, laughing.

But I knew his heart and I knew his wishes, and I prayed every day that when the Lord took him home, it would be instantaneously—right into Jesus' loving arms.

That's exactly what happened. When I first saw Frank lying on the floor, his eyes were wide open in astonishment as if he'd suddenly seen something amazing. Because he had.

I believe Frank saw Jesus, and Jesus took his breath away.

Isaiah 61:1–3 says:

He has sent me to bind up the brokenhearted . . .

and provide for those who grieve in Zion—

to bestow on them a crown of beauty

instead of ashes,

the oil of joy

instead of mourning,

and a garment of praise

instead of a spirit of despair.

They will be called oaks of righteousness,

a planting of the LORD

for the display of his splendor.

All of us who loved Frank beyond words experienced this same joy and peace and comfort on that day and in the days that came after.

People would say, "I'm so sorry you lost your husband." And I would always reply: "Oh, he isn't lost. I know exactly where he is."

How could we all have this otherworldly, supernatural, doesn't-make-any-human-sense joy? Because we all know Jesus personally, and His promises to us are real and His Word is true.

We know we will all see Frank again someday. And I will see my father and mother and everyone else who has passed on to glory through their faith in Jesus, the Messiah.

This is only the beginning, and there will be no end.

So I encourage you to find your stone and throw it at the chaos of this world. Serve the living God and find your purpose in Him. Rejoice in hope and overflow with joy. Lift up your hands and worship Him in spirit and truth with awe and wonder. Sing praises to His name and cast your crowns at His feet. And thank Him that you are like "an olive tree flourishing in the house of God; I trust in God's unfailing love for ever and ever" (Psalm 52:8).

Amen.

On June 16, 2017, I had the great joy of meeting Brett James in Nashville. Brett is one of the most successful songwriters in country music, and together we wrote this song about Frank's passing.

HE SAW JESUS

A little kiss, a little coffee, a little moment to pray.
Our Sunday mornings always started that way.
Makeup in the mirror, hummin' a gospel song.
When I came down the stairs I knew something was wrong.
He was lyin' on the floor. He was in a better place,
And I could tell for sure by that sweet look on his face . . .

[Chorus]
He saw Jesus. He saw Jesus.
And He took his breath away.
He was a man who never wanted to leave his house,
But he went home that day.
He saw the heavens open,
Saw the Father's open arms.
When you see that kind of love, how could you stay?
He saw Jesus. He saw Jesus,
And He took his breath away.

No, I didn't lose him. I know right where he is.
See, he was never really mine. He was always His.
And tho I miss his kisses, and I can't fill the empty space,
It helps when I remember that sweet look on his face when . . .

[Repeat chorus]

Now I know every Sunday morning when I kneel down to pray,
He'd want me to live, he'd want me to love, each and every day,
'Til I see Jesus, I see Jesus and He takes my breath away.
I'm in no hurry to leave this world behind,
But I know I'll go to a better place.
I'll see the heavens open, see the Father's open arms,
And when I feel that kind of love what can I say
But thank You, Jesus, thank You, Jesus, as You take my breath
  away.
So I'll keep breathing, I'll keep breathing,
'Til He takes my breath away.

AFTERWORD

It is the last day before this manuscript is due to the publisher. I am filled with a sense of wonderful relief that we have made the deadline, and yet a tangible anxiety nips at the edges of my mind: Did I get everything right? Did I acknowledge every source properly? Did I leave anything out that could truly bless or persuade or explain better what I long to share of my love of the Rock, the Road, and the Rabbi?

The answers to these questions are: no, hopefully, and probably!

As much as I long to understand what the words in Scripture mean, I don't agonize over the things I don't understand. There is much you just can't Google to get an answer for or you get so many divergent answers that you're more confused than when you initially asked the question.

So I embrace the miracles, the majesty, and the mystery of the Bible. I love the Scripture that says: "Now we see things imperfectly, like puzzling reflections in a mirror, but then we will see everything with perfect clarity. All that I know now is partial and incomplete, but then I will know everything completely, just as God now knows me completely" (1 Corinthians 13:12 NLT).

What a relief! And what a glorious "hope and future" awaits us (Jeremiah 29:11)!

And my favorite: "Eye has not seen, nor ear heard, nor have entered into the heart of man the things which God has prepared for those who love Him" (1 Corinthians 2:9 NKJV).

As I close this book, I rest in the assurance of Romans 8:28: "All things work together for good to those who love God, to those who are the called according to His purpose" (NKJV).

God, who knows me and loves me anyway, will forgive my shortcomings, my mistakes, and my misguided good intentions. He has done so every day of my life.

He knows my heart, and He forgets all my iniquities. Therefore, I will hit the Send button and trust that He will use this flawed effort to help bring His *shalom* to the chaos of this world. This world He created. This world full of people and creatures He loves. This world He died for, and this world He is yet coming to redeem.

Shalom Shalom
—Kathie Lee
Greenwich, Connecticut
June 30, 2017

Next year in Jerusalem!

APPENDIX

The Rock and Road Experience

What joy for those whose strength comes from the LORD,
who have set their minds on a pilgrimage to Jerusalem.

—PSALM 84:5 NLT

In October 2016, a group of fifty seminarians, messianic students, and pastors from The King's University in Dallas, Texas, traveled to Israel for a Rock and Road Experience—a Bible study tour of Israel led by Rod and Libby Van Solkema. They were the first of what I hope will result in similar groups setting out every week from every state in America to study the rabbinic way in the Holy Land.

My prayer is that evangelical Christians and Jews will agree to sponsor and fund these trips in order to bless them, and to bless Israel as well, filling planes and buses and hotels and mountaintops with seekers of deeper truth in their spiritual journeys.

Many of my Israeli friends tell me the only true friends Israel has are American evangelical Christians, because we love the Rock

(Jesus), the Road (the Holy Land), and the Rabbi (the Word of God). And we love the Jewish people. And, by the way, because of the teachings of Jesus, we also love everyone else who lives in the land.

How glorious would it be to go and then sponsor someone on such a trip? This is how we can impact the kingdom exponentially.

The first fifty will return and bring fifty others, who will return with others until one day, Lord willing, a Rock and Road Experience group will be on the Mount of Olives when the Lord Jesus Himself returns to the very spot!

Zechariah 14:4 tells us, "On that day his feet will stand on the Mount of Olives, east of Jerusalem, and the Mount of Olives will be split in two from east to west, forming a great valley, with half of the mountain moving north and half moving south."

ROCK AND ROAD EXPERIENCE
TESTIMONIALS

There were so many lessons that impacted my faith during our trip to the Holy Land, but my biggest takeaway was the importance of relying on the body of Christ. During the second day of our trip I took a fall that resulted in a ligament tear in my left ankle. Being a former Special Forces medic, I knew the injury was serious. I had to make a decision to stay and push through, or head home. I decided, "This is a once-in-a-lifetime opportunity; therefore I'll endure the discomfort to continue the journey!" For the remainder of the trip my team/family encouraged and helped me along the way. Some helped me up mountains, Vicki gave me one of her walking sticks,

Rod and Kathie and many others prayed for me, Cody checked on me constantly, and Joe (who is also a former Navy SEAL) lifted my spirits by making lighthearted fun of me. By the end of the trip, I knew that there was no way I could have made it through on my own. As I was taught in the SEAL teams, I needed to rely on teamwork to accomplish the goal, and during the trip that lesson was further reinforced.

The Rock and Road Experience strengthened me as a teammate and reminded me of the importance of relying on my community, the body of Christ, and because of that I am greatly appreciative of Kathie and the Rock and Road Experience.

— REMI ADELEKE

We had the very good fortune of having Ray, Rod, and Jason as spiritual leaders during our multiple times in Israel. We learned a lot from each of them, even though individually they had a slightly different perspective.

Being in Israel brings the Bible to life. We truly feel like we walked in the footsteps of Abraham, David, John the Baptist, and most importantly Jesus. We felt the emotions Abraham must have experienced ending up in the Zin desert while obeying God's directive to walk almost 1,400 miles to arrive there. While in En Gedi, we could almost hear David expressing his beautiful thoughts, which he later wrote in the book of Psalms. Words cannot begin to express the emotions both of us felt at being baptized again in the Jordan River near where we believe John baptized Jesus. As we walked through the poppies and olive trees in the Garden of Gethsemane, we could almost feel the weight of the world and the pain upon Jesus' shoulders as He prayed on the night of His betrayal.

We are indebted that our visits to Israel have aided our continuous journey to grow closer to Christ and God!

We wish you God's blessing!

— KAREN AND WAYLAND

Unbeknownst to me when I asked to join the tour to Israel, it would change my life forever.

I walked the path of Jesus and became closer to God. I understand the Bible more from walking the path of Jesus' life. It brought it all to life for me. I could visualize all the stories in the Bible. I will forever feel connected to each person on the trip. I have many fond memories: riding the elevator with Blakely on the first night of the trip, walking the snake trail (Masada) with Rocky, the day we spent in Caesarea Maritima and Rod's moving story about his friend, and walking through the Hasmonean Aqueduct made me believe I can do anything! I will always be thankful to have met the group of strong women on this trip and shared this experience together. I will remember Rod on the edge of every rock formation, sharing all his knowledge of the Bible, thinking he was going to fall over the edge (though he was protected). Libby telling me we were going to be friends. Without a doubt meeting my roommate Stephanie, and my bus partners, Susan and Lisa.

I do not think life is an accident. God has a plan for all His sheep. Kathie Lee was the shepherd who brought us all together.

I'm forever grateful to you, Kathie.

— MARY CASALINO

The images that you may have in your mind of the Bible are brought to life by the Road that is Israel. My pilgrimage to Israel strengthened my convictions, solidified the cracks that I had created in my own faith, and ultimately brought me closer to the Rock that is Jesus Christ.

Jesus saved my soul years ago; however, in Israel, He took a broken believer and pieced that believer back together. He showed me all the answers I had been looking for and knocked down walls that I had spent years building. Aside from the growth in my personal relationship with the Rock, Jesus restored my faith in humanity. I now see God and Jesus more completely and more fully. I see His plan for mankind. I am forever grateful for my opportunity to explore this land with some of the people I love most.

My hope, in this little testimony, is that anyone on the fence about going to Israel or on the fence about their own personal faith might take the next step and reach out to our Rock. He is waiting patiently.

— CHRISTIANA GIFFORD

Picture in your mind an entire country the size of New Jersey. That's Israel—263 miles from north to south and 71 miles from east to west. Jesus' footprints covered an incredibly small square footage when you think about the impact He made across the world and for so many generations.

The landscape of Israel was unlike anything I had expected. Israel is a beautiful country, stretching from mountains to desert to rivers and seas. On our second day, we made our way into the Israeli Zin desert, where the Israelites spent most of their forty years of wandering; the two days spent there were enlightening to my spirit. It's easy to view the desert as barren, arid land where very little could grow, much less thrive, but I learned that the desert shaped the story of God's people. When He leads you into a spiritual desert, it's to draw you away from the distractions and noise of a fruitful land, and into a space that requires dependence and focus on Him alone.

The Bible refers to the desert more than any other physical place. Most of us are familiar with the Israelites' forty years of wandering through the dusty, mountainous, sandy terrain—their conversations full of grumbling, complaining, and doubting the God who had led them out of slavery in a miraculous show of protection and provision. They felt lost and stranded as they wandered deeper and deeper into the deserted unknown. What they (and we!) failed to realize, is that God didn't just deliver them from their captors and take His hands off, but He led them into the desert and continued to be their guide for those forty years, ultimately leading them directly into the Promised Land flowing with milk and honey. As we feel the temperatures and heat rise around us, when we're in the middle of fiery trials, it is imperative that we press into a God who provides and protects us, and who is leading us through the deserts and into His promised land of riches and glory.

As we trekked through the Zin desert and worked our way across the rocky landscape, we saw movement above us on the mountain. We realized that the movement was the agile balancing of small deer (they looked like goats in our eyes) nimbly traversing their environment. We watched them in amazement as we read the Scripture in Habakkuk about God equipping His people with the feet of the deer.

My time in the desert (literally) will forever change the way I prepare my heart for my times in the desert (figuratively). Rather than plead with God to deliver me out of the deserts He leads me into, I will recognize that when He draws me away from my place of comfort, it is to speak to me intimately and in silence . . . in His Holiest of Holies. Second, my prayers will receive a transformative renovation.

Rather than praying that God would take the desert away from me, I will pray like Habakkuk that instead, God would give me the feet of the deer to equip me to traverse the desert well.

—ANNE NEILSON

Our journey to the Holy Land began with an inauspicious initial destination: Hadassah Hospital. Considering Mom is the Energizer Bunny incarnate, it comes as no real surprise that she occasionally overexerts herself; and the first morning of our trip to Israel proved to be no different.

A powerful combination of jet lag, hitting the ground running, and shooting for *Today* at the Western Wall had led to some understandable fatigue (she'd kill me if I said "age-related" fatigue—so I'll hope this escapes her finely tuned editorial eye). Not one to miss the party, however, Mom marched forward bravely, leading our group full steam ahead into the beautifully vibrant Israeli countryside. She performed her leadership function admirably, until I realized that she was nowhere to be found—and attendance is something of a leadership prerequisite.

Unbeknownst to me, our human Energizer Bunny had suffered a mild case—she'd refute this diagnosis, but no one ever questioned her flare for the dramatic!—of heat exhaustion, and was resting comfortably at the bottom of a lush hillside as our group took in the stunning vista of the ancient Via Maris defining the Mediterranean coastline to the West.

As mere precaution, we escorted her to Hadassah Hospital to confirm everything was in working order. One of my most memorable experiences occurred shortly thereafter, and that was bearing witness to the incredible professionalism and unity displayed by a diverse multicultural staff at Israel's busiest healing center. From beginning to end, Christians, Jews, and Muslims worked together around the clock to ensure that my mother received world-class care.

In a region of the world often criticized for its cultural, ethnic, and religious divisions, what I witnessed was nothing short of God's mercy working through His children—irrespective of where they hailed from or what beliefs they subscribed to.

James 1:17 tells us, "Every good and perfect gift is from above, coming down from the Father of the heavenly lights, who does not change like shifting shadows." My first impression of Israel, therefore, was an unexpected yet mighty display of these perfect gifts. The kind words of a stranger. The quiet patience of a doctor. And the love for one's neighbor—especially for those seemingly different than ourselves.

— CODY GIFFORD

Walking the Bible, step by step from Old Testament to New Testament, made my religious education come to life! To stand on a spot and realize there are twenty-seven layers of history underfoot and that a stone bearing the engraving, "Entry to Solomon's Kingdom" had just been unearthed at bottom; to sail across the Sea of Galilee and walk the streets of Capernaum where Jesus ministered; and to take bread and wine in the Garden of Gethsemane while looking across at the Temple Mount, all while reading the Scripture and touching these places intimately as Thomas touched the wounds of Jesus . . . I cried tears of relief and revelation on a level that it is hard to find words to explain. I wish this gift, this grace to every being on earth.

— KELLY YAEGERMANN

There aren't enough words to describe the life-changing impact of my trip to Israel. It was refreshing. It was enlightening. It was powerful. I studied in the Holy Land during a time of my life where I was seeking direction from God. Immediately, He began to speak to me through our dynamic leaders, Rod and Libby, the land we explored, and our team members. Every day was like drinking the most refreshing cup of water. I always wanted more because it was something I had never experienced before.

Your life will be transformed after studying in the Holy Land. The Gospel stories will come alive in new and unusual ways. Your relationship with Jesus will never be the same.

— KYLE MICHAEL MILLER

I was honored to be a part of Kathie Lee's Rock and Road Experience in Israel last year. Aside from our having a chance to sing the songs we had written in various biblical settings (surreal and thrilling, to say the least), having been raised in the Jewish faith, I got a much more profound understanding of how the Old and New Testaments worked together.

As a result of climbing Israel's extraordinary mountains, bathing in its rivers, and traversing its ancient deserts, I experienced a renewed and quietly personal connection with God and my own spiritual nature. In terms of Jesus Himself, I was blown away to learn of His unflinching bravery and willingness to speak His powerful truths directly into the faces of the Roman and religious hierarchy of the day. Where most spiritual teachers through the centuries would cloister themselves away in some holy place and have their students come to them to "sit at the hem of their garment," not Jesus. He brought His message of love for one's fellows and of being living messengers of God's love to everyone everywhere and risked life and limb to do so.

My gratitude, respect, and love for Him is boundless, and I thank

Kathie Lee, Rod, Libby, and the others for this indescribable and unforgettable experience.

—DAVID POMERANZ
Award-winning recording artist and songwriter

On our last night in Israel, I was quite simply overwhelmed with the goodwill and beautiful spirit of my new family, the wonderful group I had been privileged to travel the Holy Land with. When I saw Kathie Lee at dinner I just had to say, "I think you brought me here to learn about Christ and what it means to be a Christian. But now that I have been here, I really think I want to be Jewish." Of course, she had the best answer anyone could give. She said, "The good news is that you can be both!"

I had arrived in Israel with, what I learned, one might call a "mustard seed" of faith. I knew that I had also brought a mountain of doubt in my carry-on. Learning about Judeo-Christian history and culture helped me see that "faith" is exactly as improbable as it sounds. To me, faith is an openness of the heart to allow the wonders in. Of course, being me, I still question everything, but that little seed is planted deeply. I believe that God loves every one of us, even the reluctant.

—VICTORIA KENNEDY

On October 28, 2016, I arrived in the land of Israel with approximately fifty other individuals. The group was comprised of pastors, faculty, and students from The King's University. Over an eleven-day span, we ate, rode the tour bus, and hiked a total of eighty-five miles together. It was a beautiful experience to observe God's people coming together to learn more about the Bible, the land, the people, and ourselves.

One of my most memorable events occurred on the third day, when the group climbed the mountain fortress of Masada. It was here where God spoke to me through Psalm 119:105, which declares, "Your word is a lamp for my feet, a light on my path." As I ascended Masada with the others, I began to better comprehend that this spiritual journey can only be accomplished one step at a time. It requires patience, perseverance, and a strong walk with God if I am to finish this race. However, I cannot become so concerned about my own spiritual well-being that I forget to acknowledge the wounded standing on the side of the mountain. Helping my fellow brothers reach the summit of Masada gave me the greatest joy because no one was left behind.

This trip and specifically this event changed my life because I began to realize it doesn't matter how fast I run, the most important goal is ensuring all of God's children finish the race.

— TERRY JACKSON

Walking the ancient paths in Israel was an experience like none other in my life. The atmosphere as well as the terrain exudes God's story wrought and etched in the fabric of the land. Walking in the footsteps of our predecessors in the faith was not only a journey in time but also a journey within.

Having served in ministry over four decades, I came to the Holy Land at the end of my own wilderness. Unbeknownst to me, God was both escorting me and awaiting my presence in specific places: the Jericho road, the caves of Adullam, and ultimately the desert. Upon the same fierce landscapes that Abraham's, Moses', and David's scorched souls encountered the living God, He was faithful to meet me in my own raw vulnerability.

What was said of Him is true: "A bruised reed he will not break, and a smoldering wick he will not snuff out" (Isaiah 42:3).

— ANONYMOUS

Being in Israel was a life-changing experience. Seeing the Scripture come to life, experiencing the land Jesus walked, and touching the promises of God is indescribable. I am more in love with the Lord and His Word than I could ever imagine, a love that grows in revelation of Him daily, through His Word and through His land.

Experiencing Israel gave me new eyes to "see" His Scripture through God's lens—His perspective—and removed the cultural blindness of my Western world lens.

— SARAH SANDERS

Visiting the land of Israel is stepping into a pivotal place in history, the present, and the days to come. Israel holds utmost importance for understanding the God of the Bible. It is also a fundamental location of world history and modern technology. It stands in the center of global politics.

Israel has something to offer everyone. Whether the feel of the ancient stones, the aroma of spices in the markets, the breathtaking sunsets over the sea of Galilee, or the feeling of arriving at an ancient homeland, Israel is a place that once experienced will never be forgotten.

— SHAWN MOIR

I was not supposed to be on this, my first, trip to Israel, but God . . .

Israel changed me in more ways than a brief story can tell. It has had a way of flowing to the plethora of deep places in my life and overflowing every valley.

Two important events occurred. First, praying at the Kotel connected me to Jewish people in an unusually significant way, where our prayers and the presence of God blended in a beautiful cacophony. Second, I told God that because a Christian in a high place blessed me, I wanted to be a blessing to another and He could use me. On the way home during the layover in San Francisco, Sarah and I met Chuck Norris and his wife, and I asked if I could pray for them. Coincidentally, they were on their way to Israel.

— KIM BEARD

On the fourth day of our trip that Kathie Lee had so graciously donated, our guide affectionately known as Rabbi Coach Rod (Rod Van Solkema) led us up a rocky road to a mountain, which many believe was the mountain where Moses received the Ten Commandments. At its crest, there was a wide, open area where our team of weary sojourners could spread out (at the encouragement of Rod) to pray and seek the God of Israel. I positioned myself behind a large rock and cried out to the Lord for the salvation of His people and His land that His Word so often attributes as key to the restoration of the world.

God never abandons those with whom He starts. Behind the rock, I had a unique sense of proximity to the divine presence as I cried out to God for all Israel "to hear" and "love the LORD" as Deuteronomy 6 states, and as the Rabbi *Yeshua* (Jesus) taught and emulated (Matthew 22:37; Luke 13:34). Hearing God's voice was distinctive for Moses on the mount then, as His voice is distinctive for all who have an intimate relationship with Him today (Hebrews 3:13–15; Psalm 95:7–8).

I will never be the same.

— J. AXTELL

Life is not a straight line! From October 27 to November 8, 2016, an unexpected change occurred in my life that caused the linear path I was on to take a turn, shall we say? There's the saying, "Life events happen"—i.e., death of a loved one, birth of a child, et al. However, toward the winding down of year 2016, a Tuesday night, before retiring to bed, while checking email, I discovered an unusual subject line: "You have been invited." I was a student—one of a group of fifty— chosen to travel to the Holy Land in an all-expenses-paid trip to Israel gifted by a philanthropist! We would go on the Rock and Road Experience, hiking the mountains of Israel.

Although there were many sacred and holy occurrences that happened there, I'd rather share a page out of my journal that I wrote upon returning home to Detroit, Michigan, that sums it up better.

November 9, 2016

To My Bet-Av Fam! I think I'm the last to get back home: Deee-troit!!

We climbed Masada! *(hard)*

We climbed Mt. Sinai! *(strenuous/arduous)*

We climbed Mt. Arbel! *(rocky)*

We climbed Mt. Olivet! *(very vertical)*

We climbed Jericho! *(steep/steep)*

We climbed foothills! (felt like mountains . . . LOL!)

We crouched down w/ flashlights into caves!

We partook of communion together!

We hiked the "hot desert" together!

We cooled off in En Gedi together!

We swam together in the Dead Sea at night, floating, gazing at the stars! *(so fun)*

We had conversations about a lady who interrupted our lives—
Kathie Lee Gifford!

We cried together!

We encouraged together!

We prophesied to one another and together!

We prayed for one another!

We prayed for each other's families!

We prayed for each other's fears!

We even disagreed w/ one another!

We walked through Jaffa Gate together!

We experienced countless, beautiful hotels together! *(7 to be exact!)* Wow!

We spent 12 days together!

We spent 2 days of travel together!

We've walked Israel together! *(beautiful land) (God's land!)*

We were from every race and ethnic group: African American, Aussies, Chinese, Jewish, Caucasians, Scottish, et al. . . . but we became Bet-Av—family.

— JODI A. MATTHEWS
The King's University student, Jewish Messianic Studies Program

Israel rocked my soul.

Aside from frequently feeling inspired by Kathie's stories about her own time in the Holy Land, prior to arriving there myself I didn't know exactly what to expect.

Despite the various conflicts surrounding Israel, the land has remained one of the most beautiful and often undisturbed places—consisting of some of the warmest people I've ever met.

I will never forget the immense sense of peace I felt while traveling through the different cities and regions in Israel, and even more significantly, how much His presence seemed to permeate the entire land. The very last day of our journey, after having heard about all of the recent archaeological discoveries such as the Seal of Hezekiah uncovered in the ancient City of David, we met an Israeli tour guide who concluded the trip with a profound message. This enchanting young woman shared with us how "She"—meaning Israel—is getting ready for our Savior's return. "She is getting ready." I am too.

— ERIKA BROWN

This walk through Israel took me from chaos, which we spoke of often, to peace. When standing on the ground where David probably stood as he slew Goliath, where Jesus wept the night He was arrested, where the tablets were found, I saw with my own eyes how real this history is.

I had my birthday with my new friends in a boat on the Sea of Galilee, where Jesus appeared walking on water to His friends He loved. I saw how close we were traveling into the real history of the beginnings of our Christ. We got up each day with a group that started as strangers, who through morning prayer became our cohesive insula, and together we took the same journey as Christ's forebears. All this made the holy days of Easter much more as I returned home to Washington.

— BOBBI SMITH

Stop me if you've heard this one: A Hindu, a Sikh, and a group of Catholics and Christians head to Israel. . . .

Sure, it sounds like the start of a weird joke. But for me, Israel was a longtime dream. Growing up in Israel West—also known as northern New Jersey—I always imagined going to the Promised Land. I had always felt there was an energy in the land that was connected to my own, and the two times my husband and I tried to make the trip, Middle Eastern travel restrictions prevented us from going.

Fast-forward a few years, and Kathie Lee Gifford invited my husband and me on a trip she was putting together with her friends and family. I immediately said yes. My husband, Agan, had a previous work commitment he couldn't bail on, so I decided to go alone. But as she does, Kathie said she'd pray on it. And if you don't know—when Kathie Lee prays, things start to happen. Within weeks, Agan's long-standing work trip was canceled, and the two of us were heading to Israel together; our baby daughter would stay with my parents.

The first time I read the story of David and Goliath, we were sitting on rocks in the Valley of Elah. And the first time I read David's Psalms about living water, his thirst for God, and his confidence in being guided by his Shepherd despite being aggressively hunted by Saul, we were in En Gedi, the cool water falling freely in the middle of the dry, cracked desert. I had never read the Bible before, and the stories were literally coming to life, right in front of our eyes. And it was clear—like so many things in Israel—this wasn't an accident. It was divine order.

As we lay in bed at night, Agan and I talked about the day, the walk, the stones. We had conversations we'd never even considered before, thoughts and prayers fueled by the teachings or readings of the day. The truth is, we had cleared some rocky terrain in our marriage already—our infant daughter was diagnosed with and beat cancer before her first birthday. And it was impossible not to see the parallels—the signs that were placed all over the land, seemingly just for us, to remind us that we were going the right way, in life, with each other, always guided by a guide. The Guide.

We left Israel different than when we arrived—still Sikh, still Hindu—but with Shema on our lips and in our hearts, with a deep gratitude for Israel and all her lessons. And our marriage was stronger because of it.

For us, the Promised Land had kept its promise, and then some.

— RAAKHEE MIRCHANDANI

NOTES

INTRODUCTION
1. John J. Parsons, "The Awe of the Lord," hebrew4christians.com/
Scripture/Parashah/Summaries/Eikev/Yirah/yirah.html.
2. Ibid.
3. Ibid.

MEET THE GOOD RABBI: JASON SOBEL
1. Babylonian Talmud, Sanhedrin 99a.

CHAPTER 5: CAESAREA AND HERODIUM
1. Flavius Josephus, *Antiquities of the Jews*, Book XVII, translation available
at sacred-texts.com/jud/josephus/ant-17.htm.
2. Dean Smith, "Tomb of Herod the Great Discovered,"
OpenTheWord.org, April 24, 2017, opentheword.org/2017/04/24/
tomb-of-herod-the-great-discovered/.
3. Flavius Josephus, *Antiquities of the Jews*, Book XV, translation available at
penelope.uchicago.edu/josephus/ant-15.html.
4. Flavius Josephus, *The Wars of the Jews*, Book I, translation available at
sacred-texts.com/jud/josephus/war-1.htm.

CHAPTER 6: BETHLEHEM
1. Mishnah Shekalim 7:4.

CHAPTER 7: NAZARETH
1. Talmud, Babylonian Sukkah 52.

2. "Inflection of *tzel*," pealim.com, pealim.com/dict/4242-tzel/.

CHAPTER 9: THE SEVEN STREAMS

1. Oppians, *Halieutica or Fishing*, translation available at penelope.uchicago. edu/Thayer/E/Roman/Texts/Oppian/Halieutica/1.html.

CHAPTER 11: CAPERNAUM

1. Amir Tsarfati, "Ancient Synagogue Where Jesus Taught Discovered in Galilee," *Kehila News Israel*, August 16, 2016, kehilanews.com/2016/08/16/ ancient-synagogue-where-jesus-taught-discovered-in-galilee/.

CHAPTER 16: THE POOL OF SILOAM

1. Bible Archaeology Society Staff, "The Siloam Pool: Where Jesus Healed the Blind Man," *Bible History Daily*, July 2, 2017, biblicalarchaeology. org/daily/biblical-sites-places/biblical-archaeology-sites/ the-siloam-pool-where-jesus-healed-the-blind-man/.

2. Ibid.

3. Babylonian Talmud, Bava Batra 126b.

CHAPTER 18: THE MOUNT OF OLIVES

1. Rick Westhead, "Jerusalem's Mount of Olives Cemetery Running Out of Room," *Toronto Star*, December 16, 2012, thestar.com/news/ world/2012/12/16/jerusalems_mount_of_olives_cemetery_running_ out_of_room.html.

CHAPTER 22: GOLGOTHA

1. Dave Epstein, "Found and Lost?" in *Nelson's Annual Preacher's Sourcebook*, O. S. Hawkins, ed., vol. 3 (Nashville, TN: Thomas Nelson, 2013), 161.

2. Ibid.

CHAPTER 24: THE UPPER ROOM AND TEMPLE COURTS

1. Moshe Weinfeld, *Normative and Sectarian Judaism in the Second Temple Period* (London: T & T Clark, 2005), p. 274.

CHAPTER 26: THE DEAD SEA

1. Ezekiel 47:8–9, JPS Tanakh, Bible Hub, biblehub.com/jps/ezekiel/47. htm.
2. Samantha Siegel, "Fish Living by the Dead Sea—Prophecy of Ezekiel Unfolding," July 21, 2016, youtube.com/watch?v=x5A3GkuRaMI.
3. Adam Eliyahu Berkowitz, "Fulfillment of the Dead Sea Prophecy Has Begun," Breaking Israel News, July 27, 2016, breakingisraelnews. com/72711/fulfillment-dead-sea-prophecy-begun/#/.

CHAPTER 27: MASADA

1. Aviva and Shmuel Bar-Am, "Masada, Tragic Fortress in the Sky," *Times of Israel*, April 13, 2013, timesofisrael.com/ masada-tragic-fortress-in-the-sky/.
2. Flavius Josephus, *The Wars of the Jews*, Book VII, chapter 9, translation available at sacred-texts.com/jud/josephus/war-7.htm.

CHAPTER 28: THE QUMRAN CAVES

1. Jewish Virtual Library, jewishvirtuallibrary.org/ teacher-of-righteousness.
2. Jeffrey L. Sheler, "The Reason God Tested Abraham," *U.S. News and World Report*, June 29, 1997, money.usnews.com/money/ personal-finance/articles/1997/06/29/the-reason-god-tested-abraham.

CHAPTER 29: TEL AVIV

1. Henry Alford, "Seizing the Day in Tel Aviv," *New York Times*, July 20, 2008, www.nytimes.com/2008/07/20/travel/20telaviv.html.

CONCLUSION

1. "Watch Kathie Lee's Touching Tribute to Husband Frank Gifford," Today.com, August 17, 2015, www.today.com/video/watch-kathie- lees-touching-tribute-to-husband-frank-gifford-506707523589.

ABOUT THE AUTHORS

KATHIE LEE GIFFORD is the three-time Emmy-winning cohost of the fourth hour of *TODAY*, alongside Hoda Kotb. The Gifford-Kotb hour has been hailed as "appointment television" by *Entertainment Weekly*, and "*TODAY*'s happy hour" by *USA Today*.

Prior to NBC News, Gifford served as cohost of *Live with Regis and Kathie Lee* for fifteen years, where she received eleven Emmy nominations. She was also a correspondent for *Good Morning America* for three years. In 2015, she was inducted into the Broadcast & Cable Hall of Fame. Her Broadway musical, *Scandalous*, for which she wrote the book and the lyrics, received a Tony nomination for its lead actress. Also a songwriter, Kathie recently wrote "He Saw Jesus" and "Jesus Is His Name," as well as the score and script for the movie *A Reel Life*.

Gifford has authored three *New York Times* bestselling books, including *Just When I Thought I'd Dropped My Last Egg*, *I Can't Believe I Said That*, and the popular children's book *Party Animals*. Her book *Good Gifts: One Year In the Heart of a Home* raised over $1 million for the Salvation Army.

Gifford lends support to numerous children's organizations, including Childhelp, the Association to Benefit Children, the Salvation Army, and the International Justice Mission. A devoted humanitarian, she received an honorary degree from Marymount University for her humanitarian work in labor relations.

Gifford has two children, Cody and Cassidy, and resides in Connecticut.

About the Authors
(CONTINUED)

RABBI JASON SOBEL is a thought leader, spiritual guide, and Jewish follower of Yeshua (Jesus). He is cofounder of Fusion with Rabbi Jason, an organization dedicated to sharing teachings and resources that reveal deeper insights into the Jewish roots of the Scriptures. Learn more at www.rabbisobel.com.

JOIN RABBI JASON ON A ROCK, ROAD, AND RABBI TOUR OF ISRAEL!

Visit www.rockroadrabbitours.com to learn more about this unique experience designed around the rabbinic approach to learning and living the biblical text. A Rock, Road, and Rabbi Tour is a "Road to Emmaus" encounter—your eyes will be opened as the Old and New Testament connect in high definition.

You will never see Jesus and the Bible the same way again!

New Video Study for Your Church or Small Group

If you've enjoyed this book, now you can go deeper with the companion video Bible study!

In this six-session study, Kathie Lee Gifford helps you apply the principles in *The Rock, the Road, and the Rabbi* to your life. The study guide includes video notes, group discussion questions, and personal study and reflection materials for in-between sessions.

Study Guide
9780310095019

DVD
9780310095033

Available now at your favorite bookstore,
or streaming video on StudyGateway.com.

 Thomas Nelson
Since 1798